# 2nd International Workshop on Gender-Inclusive Translation Technologies (GITT 2024)



Sheffield, United Kingdom
27 June 2024

ISBN: 979-8-3313-0479-9

**Printed from e-media with permission by:**

Curran Associates, Inc.
57 Morehouse Lane
Red Hook, NY 12571

**Some format issues inherent in the e-media version may also appear in this print version.**



Association for Computational Linguistics
209 N. Eighth Street
Stroudsburg, Pennsylvania 18360

Phone: 1-570-476-8006
Fax: 1-570-476-0860

acl@aclweb.org

**Additional copies of this publication are available from:**

Curran Associates, Inc.
57 Morehouse Lane
Red Hook, NY 12571 USA
Phone: 845-758-0400
Fax: 845-758-2633
Email: curran@proceedings.com
Web: www.proceedings.com

GITT 2024

# 2nd International Workshop on Gender-Inclusive Translation Technologies

## Proceedings of the Workshop

June 27, 2024

The GITT organizers gratefully acknowledge the support from the following sponsors.

**Sponsors**

Google

GHENT UNIVERSITY

TILBURG UNIVERSITY

# Preface

This volume contains the proceedings of the 2nd International Workshop on Gender-Inclusive Translation Technologies (GITT 2024)[1], hosted by the 25th Annual Conference of The European Association for Machine Translation (EAMT 2024)[2]. GITT is set out to focus on gender-inclusive language in translation and cross-lingual scenarios. The workshop brings together researchers from diverse areas, including industry partners, MT practitioners and language professionals. Also, GITT aims to encourage multidisciplinary research that develops and interrogates both solutions and challenges for addressing bias and promoting gender inclusivity in MT and translation tools, including LLM applications for translation.

The workshop welcomed three types of contributions: research papers, research communications, and extended abstracts. GITT-2024 received a total of 6 novel submissions (5 research papers, 1 extended abstract) and 2 research communication. Following the review process, all 6 submissions received positive reviews, highlighting an increase in the quality of the submissions received (i.e. GITT-2023 resulted in an acceptance rate of 75%). It is worth noting that the research communications did not undergo the review process as it had previously undergone peer-review at a top-tier conference. Of the accepted papers, 4 have been assigned to oral presentations, while the remaining 1, as well as the accepted abstract, have been assigned to the poster session. The research communications, which are not included in the proceedings, are also to be presented during the poster session in order to promote dissemination of research aligned with the scope of the workshop.

The accepted papers cover a diverse range of topics related to the analysis, measurement, and mitigation of gender bias in (Machine) Translation, as well as to the investigation of inclusive language. We are glad to attest to the interdisciplinary perspectives and methods represented in GITT submissions. The contributions range from technical papers proposing novel methods to position papers, user-centric experiments on the use of inclusive language, including reflection on the translation and localization of archival data with an inclusive and historically-grounded perspective.

In addition to the technical programme, we are honoured to have four invited speakers: Kevin Robinson (Google Research), with a keynote entitled "*Multilingual gender-inclusivity in translation and beyond*"; Begoña Martínez Pagán (University of Murcia) with the keynote "*Intersectionality and gender in translation — how ethical must one automatically be?*". Finally, the program includes a panel session on "Navigating Gender Inclusivity: From Research to Professional Practice", which – on top of the invited keynote speakers – includes two additional panelists: Paula Manzur (Booking.com) and Helena Moniz (University of Lisbon, INESC-ID/Unbabel).

We sincerely thank all the people and institutions that contributed to the success of the workshop: the authors of the submitted papers for their interest in the topic; the Programme Committee members for their valuable feedback and insightful comments; the EAMT organizers for their support. Finally, we thank our sponsors, Google, the Faculty of Arts and Philosophy at Ghent University, and Tilburg University for their generous contributions.

We hope you enjoy reading the papers and are looking forward to a fruitful and enriching workshop!

*June 2024,*
*Beatrice Savoldi, Janiça Hackenbuchner, Luisa Bentivogli,*
*Joke Daems, Eva Vanmassenhove, and Jasmijn Bastings*

[1] https://sites.google.com/tilburguniversity.edu/gitt2024
[2] https://eamt2024.sheffield.ac.uk/

# Organizing Committee

## Program Chairs


Beatrice Savoldi,
*Fondazione Bruno Kessler (FBK), Trento, Italy*

Janiça Hackenbuchner,
*Department Translation, Interpreting and Communication, Ghent University, Ghent, Belgium*

Luisa Bentivogli,
*Fondazione Bruno Kessler (FBK), Trento, Italy*

Joke Daems,
*Department Translation, Interpreting and Communication, Ghent University, Ghent, Belgium*

Eva Vanmassenhove,
*Department Cognitive Science and Artificial Intelligence, School of Humanities and Digital Sciences, Tilburg University (TiU), Tilburg, The Netherlands*

Jasmijn Bastings,
*Google DeepMind*

# Program Committee

## Program Committee

Dennis Fucci, Fondazione Bruno Kessler
Andrea Piergentili, University of Trento
Pushpdeep Singh, Tata Consultancy Services Limited, India
Danielle Saunders, DeepL
Jan Niehues, Karlsruher Institut für Technologie
Guillaume Wisniewski, LLF / Université Paris Cité
Anna Currey, Amazon
Beatrice Spallaccia, University of Bologna
Manuel Lardelli, Universität Graz
Gabriel Stanovsky, Hebrew University of Jerusalem
Nizar Habash, New York University Abu Dhabi
María Isabel Rivas Ginel, Dublin City University
Michal Měchura, Dublin City University
Johanna Monti, University of Naples L'Orientale
Matúš Pikuliak, Kempelen Institute of Intelligent Technologies
Ranjita Naik, Microsoft
Hannah Devinney, Umea University
Giuseppe Attanasio, Instituto de Telecomunicações

## Invited Speakers

Kevin Robinson, Google DeepMind
Begoña Martínez Pagán, University of Murcia

## Panelists

Paula Manzur, Booking.com
Helena Moniz, School of Arts and Humanities, University of Lisbon
Kevin Robinson, Google DeepMind
Begoña Martínez Pagán, University of Murcia

## Keynote Talk

# Multilingual gender-inclusivity in translation and beyond

**Kevin Robinson**
Google DeepMind

**Abstract:** Multilingual capabilities are increasingly available in general-purpose systems, rather than from dedicated MT systems alone. This shift impacts many practical concerns for improving gender inclusivity such as understanding downstream developer usage patterns, improving the validity of upstream evaluations, and scaling to global cultural contexts. It also raises sociotechnical research challenges in creating new kinds of transparently multilingual user experiences, improving controllability of gender-inclusive representations, and enabling new modalities like multilingual image understanding and audio generation. I discuss empirical work to measure potential misgendering harms in PaLM 2, and share experiences from more recent research at Google.

**Bio:** Kevin Robinson is a Senior Research Engineer at Google, working on developing new techniques for inclusive, controllable, and robust machine learning systems by effectively blending technical and sociocultural perspectives. Kevin has worked on research efforts like PaLM, PaLM-FLAN and PaLM 2, and contributed to products like Bard and Gemini. Kevin has separately co-authored publications on language models related to pre-training data, synthetic data generation, and measuring misgendering harms in translation systems. He is currently focused on measuring cultural and representational harms in ways that incorporate community-informed perspectives. Kevin has also worked as a special education teacher, and a computer science education researcher at MIT focused on bias within CS classrooms.

## Keynote Talk

# Intersectionality and gender in translation — how ethical must one automatically be?

**Begoña Martinez Pagan**
University of Murcia

**Abstract:** To which extent should ethical considerations inform (automated) inclusive translation processes? This talk will present a reflection on criteria for the minimum requirements of translation ethics that could be applied systematically to any text, from the point of view of intersectional, queer and feminist principles. By critically examining the ethical dimensions of translation through these lenses, this talk will seek to illuminate the path toward more inclusive, equitable, and socially responsible translation practices.

**Bio:** Begoña Martínez Pagán is a translator, interpreter, and author based at the English Studies Department of the University of Murcia. Her activism, lecturing, and research include intersections of her profession with feminist and LGBTIQ+ literature, inclusive language, human rights, business organization, and open-source software.

# Table of Contents

# Program

**Thursday, June 27, 2024**

09:00 - 09:15 *Opening Remarks*

09:15 - 10:15 *Keynote 1 (Kevin Robinson, Google DeepMind): Multilingual gender-inclusivity in translation and beyond*

10:15 - 10:30 *Poster Boaster*

10:30 - 11:00 *Coffee Break*

11:00 - 12:30 *Oral Presentations*

*Gender Bias Evaluation in Machine Translation for Amharic, Tigrigna, and Afaan Oromoo*
Walelign Tewabe Sewunetie, Atnafu Lambebo Tonja, Tadesse Destaw Belay, Hellina Hailu Nigatu, Gashaw Kidanu Gebremeskel, Zewdie Mossie, Hussien Seid and Seid Muhie Yimam

*Lost in Translation? Approaches to Gender Representation in Multilingual Archives*
Mrinalini Luthra and Brecht Nijman

*Gender and bias in Amazon review translations: by humans, MT systems and ChatGPT*
Maja Popovic and Ekaterina Lapshinova-Koltunski

*Sparks of Fairness: Preliminary Evidence of Commercial Machine Translation as English-to-German Gender-Fair Dictionaries*
Manuel Lardelli, Timm Dill, Giuseppe Attanasio and Anne Lauscher

12:30 - 13:30 *Lunch*

13:30 - 14:30 *Keynote 2 (Begoña Martínez Pagán, University of Murcia): Intersectionality and gender in translation — how ethical must one automatically be?*

14:30 - 15:30 *Poster Session*

*You Shall Know a Word's Gender by the Company it Keeps: Comparing the Role of Context in Human Gender Assumptions with MT*
Janiça Hackenbuchner, Joke Daems, Arda Tezcan and Aaron Maladry

*Building Bridges: A Dataset for Evaluating Gender-Fair Machine Translation into German*
Manuel Lardelli, Giuseppe Attanasio and Anne Lauscher

**Thursday, June 27, 2024 (continued)**

| | |
|---|---|
| | *Hi Guys or Hi Folks? Towards Gender-Neutral Machine Translation*<br>Andrea Piergentili, Beatrice Savoldi, Dennis Fucci, Matteo Negri and Luisa Bentivogli |
| | *Pilot testing gender-inclusive translations and machine translations for German quadball referee certification test takers*<br>Joke Daems |
| 15:00 - 15:30 | *Coffee Break* |
| 15:30 - 17:00 | *Panel: Navigating Gender Inclusivity: From Research to Professional Practice* |
| 17:00 - 17:00 | *Closing Remarks* |

# Gender Bias Evaluation in Machine Translation for Amharic, Tigrinya, and Afaan Oromoo

Walelign Tewabe Sewunetie[1,2], Atnafu Lambebo Tonja[3,4,5], Tadesse Destaw Belay[4], Hellina Hailu Nigatu[6], Gashaw Kidanu[7], Zewdie Mossie[1], Hussien Seid[7], Seid Muhie Yimam[8]

[∀]Ethio NLP, [1]Debre Markos University, Ethiopia, [2]University of Miskolc, Hungary, [3]Lelapa AI, [4]Instituto Politécnico Nacional, Mexico, [5]Mohamed bin Zayed University of Artificial Intelligence, UAE, [6]University of California, Berkeley, USA, [7]Addis Ababa Science and Technology University, Ethiopia [8]Universität Hamburg, Germany

## Abstract

While Machine Translation (MT) research has progressed over the years, translation systems still suffer from biases, including gender bias. While an active line of research studies the existence and mitigation strategies of gender bias in machine translation systems, there is limited research exploring this phenomenon for low-resource languages. The limited availability of linguistic and computational resources confounded with the lack of benchmark datasets makes studying bias for low-resourced languages that much more difficult. In this paper, we construct benchmark datasets to evaluate gender bias in machine translation for three low-resource languages: Afaan Oromoo (Orm), Amharic (Amh), and Tigrinya (Tir). Building on prior work, we collected 2400 gender-balanced sentences parallelly translated into the three languages. From human evaluations of the dataset we collected, we found that about 93% of Afaan Oromoo, 80% of Tigrinya, and 72% of Amharic sentences exhibited gender bias. In addition to providing benchmarks for improving gender bias mitigation research in the three languages, we hope the careful documentation of our work will help other low-resourced language researchers extend our approach to their languages.[1]



[1]Our dataset is available at https://huggingface.co/datasets/EthioNLP/Gender-Bias-Evaluation-Dataset

## 1 Introduction

Machine Translation (MT) systems play a pivotal role in breaking down language barriers and facilitating cross-cultural communication. Gender bias poses a significant challenge, particularly in languages with limited linguistic resources. The imbalance within datasets used for MT training often results in gender-related disparities. In low-resource languages like Amharic, Tigrinya, and Afaan Oromoo, and in morphologically rich languages like Arabic (Habash et al., 2019; Alhafni et al., 2022) professional names such as doctor, pilot, professor, etc., are mostly translated using the masculine gender.

Machine Translation services often default to masculine forms for professions like "doctor" and "nurse," for feminine forms potentially reflecting and reinforcing gender stereotypes. Figure 1 and Figure 2 demonstrate this for the Amharic language[2]. These types of bias can lead to misunderstandings and reinforce gender roles, influencing how people perceive different professions based on gender. Understanding and addressing gender bias in MT systems is vital for ensuring equitable and accurate communication across diverse linguistic communities.

Addressing the issue of gender bias in MT systems requires adequate datasets for evaluation; a challenging task in the context of low-resource languages. This work contributes to building equitable MT systems for low-resource languages by constructing a gold-test dataset for three languages: Amharic,

[2]In the screenshots provided, Google Translate transliterated the word "doctor" instead of translating it to the Amharic word for 'doctor' ሐኪም



*Proceedings of the 2nd International Workshop on Gender-Inclusive Translation Technologies*, pages 1–11
June 27, 2024 ©2024 European Association for Machine Translation

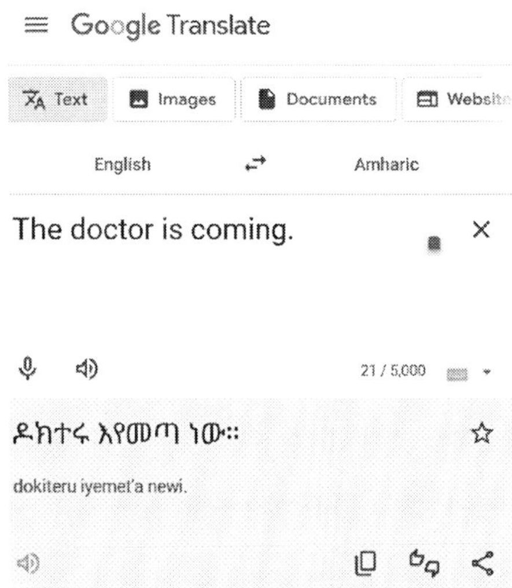


Figure 1: Translating the sentence "The doctor is coming" Google Translate translates the word "doctor" into masculine gender for the Amharic language. The word "doctor," translated in Amharic as "ዶክተር" (dokter), is gender-neutral. However, when translating "The doctor is coming," Google Translate translates the sentence to "ዶክተሩ እየመጣ ነው።" (dokteru eyemet'a new). Here the phrase "The doctor" becomes "ዶክተሩ" (dokteru); the prefix "u" indicates masculine gender in the Amharic language. In addition, the word "coming" translates into "እየመጣ" (eyemet'a); which also indicates masculine gender.

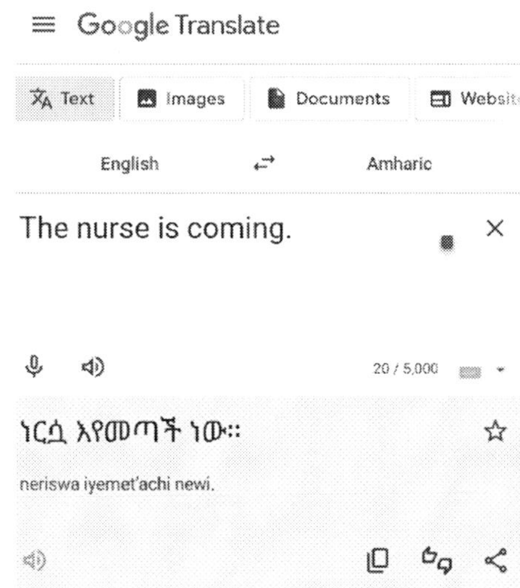


Figure 2: In the sentence "The nurse is coming", the word "nurse," translated in Amharic as "ነርስ" (ners), is gender-neutral. However, when translating "The nurse is coming," Google Translate translates the sentence to "ነርሷ እየመጣች ነው።" (nerswa eyemet'ach new). Here the phrase "The nurse" becomes "ነርሷ" (ners-wa); the prefix "wa" indicates feminine gender in the Amharic language. In addition, the word "coming" translates into "እየመጣች" (eyemet'ach); which also indicates feminine gender.

Tigrinya, and Afaan Oromoo. The methodologies developed in this research can subsequently be applied and scaled up to assess gender bias in other low-resource languages. We collected 2400 gender-balanced sentences, which can be used as a benchmark for gender bias evaluation in low-resource language translation.

In addition, this study investigates users' perceptions of gender bias in commercial MT systems and evaluates Google Translate as a use case in the three languages of study. Our analysis shows interesting differences in respondents' perceptions of gender bias across these language communities. These findings underscore the detailed relationship between language, culture, and gender bias perception in MT systems, highlighting the need for adapted approaches to mitigate bias and enhance translation accuracy within specific linguistic contexts. Furthermore, this study investigates the performance of one open-source MT model and one commercial model, namely, NLLB (Team et al., 2022), and Google MT using automatic evaluation metrics, such as SacreBleu (Post, 2018), and Chrf++ (Popović, 2017). The outcomes of this evaluation across various language pairs shed light on the efficacy and accuracy of MT systems in translating between English and the target languages. The evaluation shows diverse performance metrics across language pairs, with distinct variations in translation quality and effectiveness. These results underscore the importance of robust evaluation methodologies and metrics in assessing MT system performance and informing strategies for enhancing translation accuracy and efficiency across diverse linguistic contexts.

## 2 Related work

Investigating bias in MT systems is an active body of work in the NLP community. We use the taxonomy from (Blodgett et al., 2020a) and focus on representational harms due to stereotyping: sustaining stereotypical gender connotations for occupations during translation, thereby limiting the variety of occupations a specific gender may or may not engage in[3]. Previous works in this space have relied on (1) curating benchmark datasets (e.g.(Wairagala et al., 2022; Cho et al., 2019)), (2) human evaluation schemes (e.g. (Stanovsky et al., 2019)), and (3) automatic evaluation schemes(e.g. (Savoldi et al., 2021)). In curating benchmark datasets, (Prates et al., 2020) prepared a gender-balanced dataset for evaluating gender bias in translation systems pertaining to occupation. Since different languages represent gender in various ways (Savoldi et al., 2021), evaluation and mitigation strategies might also have to account for such variation. For instance, (Cho et al., 2019) prepared test sets with gender natural pronouns used in the Korean language for investigating bias in Korean-English translation pairs.

In evaluating gender bias in MT, several works rely on automatic metrics. (Prates et al., 2020) found that Google Translate defaults to the masculine pronoun when translating job descriptions, particularly in relation to science, technology, engineering, and mathematics (STEM) professions. (Cho et al., 2019) introduces a new evaluation index, the Translation Gender Bias Index (TGBI), for measuring gender neutrality and evaluating Korean-English translation pairs. (Stanovsky et al., 2019) introduce an evaluation protocol that relies on co-reference resolution datasets and morphological analysis to automatically evaluate gender bias across eight target languages that use grammatical gender. (Wairagala et al., 2022) used the Word Embeddings Fairness Evaluation Framework (WEFE) to measure gender bias in MT systems built for Luganda-English translation. While automated measures allow us to capture a broader understanding of the phenomenon, they may limit the detail and depth of our analysis. The study by (Stanovsky et al., 2019) uses automatic and human evaluations in tandem, exploiting both the versatility of automated evaluation and the nuance and detail captured by human evaluation.

As the work by (Blodgett et al., 2020b) argues, it is important first to articulate how bias in such systems can be harmful. Relying on the taxonomy of harms from prior work (Crawford, 2017; Barocas et al., 2017), we posit that understanding gender bias exhibited by MT systems would allow us to (1) uncover the representational harms the systems exhibit thereby understanding what power structures they uphold and (2) mitigate allocational harms that might result from deploying such systems in downstream applications (e.g. employment and job search).

One challenge in studying bias in machine-translated text is the diverse socio-cultural aspects that shape how gender is articulated among different groups and how stereotypes propagate in this diverse context. Talat et al. (2022) have shed light on the difficulty of studying and mitigating bias across multicultural, multilingual groups. Such contexts require community-rooted efforts that thoroughly investigate how the culture and language are structured. In this work, we curate benchmark datasets for three low-resource languages through collaborations among native speakers. Based on previous works, (Renduchintala et al., 2021; Stanovsky et al., 2019), we conduct an automatic evaluation of the translation quality overall and human evaluations of gender bias in popular machine translation systems to understand the current landscape of translation systems for these languages.

## 3 Background: Linguistic Gender Representation

Amharic, a Semitic language, uses grammatical gender. Most nouns and pronouns have distinct masculine and feminine forms. Gender-specific pronouns are used (e.g., **እሱ** (əssu) for "he" and **እሷ** (əsswa) for "she"), and job titles can also have gendered forms.

Like Amharic, Tigrinya, another Semitic language, has grammatical gender. Gender distinctions are marked in nouns and pronouns. There are specific pronouns for different genders (e.g., **ንሱ** (nəssu) for "he" and **ንሳ** (nəssa) for "she"), and job titles may vary depending on gender.

Afaan Oromoo, a Cushitic language, does not have grammatical gender in the same way as the other two languages. Gender-neutral pronouns are often used, but context can some-

[3] We note in this work, we are considering a binary gender system of men and women

times specify gender. Gender is less likely to be marked in job titles compared to the other two languages of study.

To illustrate more about the issues in translating a sentence and a professional word, we can see the following example of Gender Bias in English to Amharic Translation.

The English to Amharic Google Translate (accessed January 20, 2024) output of the sentence "The nurse helped the doctor" is "**ነርሷ ሐኪሙን ረድታለች።**" (nerswa hakimun redtalech). Here, "**ነርሷ**" (nerswa) 'the nurse' is female, and "**ሐኪሙን** " (hakimun) "the doctor" is male. The word "helped", while it has a translation issue[4], is translated to "**ረድታለች**" (redtalech), which is indicative of a feminine subject.

In Amharic, the source sentence "The nurse helped the doctor" can be translated in eight different ways as follows:

1. "**ነርሷ ሐኪሙን ረድታዋለች።**" (nerswa hakimun redtawalech). Here "**ነርሷ**" (neriswa) 'the nurse' is female, "**ሐኪሙን**" (hakimun) 'the doctor' is male, and "**ረድታዋለች**" (reditawalechi) 'she helped him'.

2. "**ነርሷ ሐኪሟን ረድታታለች።**" (neriswa ḥākīmwan reditatalechi). Here "**ነርሷ**" (neriswa) 'the nurse' is female, "**ሐኪሟን**" (ḥākīmwan) 'the doctor' is female, and "**ረድታታለች**" (reditatalechi) 'she helped her'.

3. "**ነርሷ ሐኪሙን ረድታቸዋለች።**" (neriswa ḥākīmun reditachewalechi) (for respect or plural). Here "**ነርሷ**" (neriswa) 'the nurse' is female, "**ሐኪሙን**" (hakimun) 'the doctor' is male, and "**ረድታቸዋለች**" (reditachewalechi) 'she helped him.'

4. "**ነርሷ ሐኪሟን ረድታቸዋለች።**" (neriswa ḥākīmwan reditachewalechi). Here "**ነርሷ**" (neriswa) 'the nurse' is female, "**ሐኪሟን**" (ḥākīmwan) 'the doctor' is female, and "**ረድታቸዋለች**" (reditachewalechi) 'she helped her' (for respect or plural).

5. "**ነርሱ ሐኪሙን ረድቶታል።**" (nersu ḥākīmun reditotale). Here "**ነርሱ**" (nersu) 'the nurse' is male, "**ሐኪሙን**" (hakimun) 'the doctor' is male, and "**ረድቶታል**" (reditotale) 'he helped him'.

6. "**ነርሱ ሐኪሟን ረድቷታል።**" (nersu ḥākīmwan reditwatale). Here "**ነርሱ**" (nersu) 'the nurse' is male, "**ሐኪሟን**" (hakimun) 'the doctor' is female, and "**ረድቷታል**" (reditwatale) 'he helped her'.

7. "**ነርሱ ሐኪሟን ረድቷቸዋል።**" (nersu ḥākīmwan reditwachewal). Here "**ነርሱ**" (nersu) 'the nurse' is male, "**ሐኪሟን**" (ḥākīmwan) 'the doctor' is female, and "**ረድቷቸዋል**" (reditwachewal) 'he helped her' (for respect or plural).

8. "**ነርሱ ሐኪሙን ረድቷቸዋል።**" (nersu ḥākīmun reditwachewal). Here "**ነርሱ**" (nersu) 'the nurse' is male, "**ሐኪሙን**" (ḥākīmun) 'the doctor' is female, and "**ረድቷቸዋል**" (reditwachewal) 'he helped him' (for respect or plural).

This range of translations reflects the potential for gender bias in translation when assumptions are made about the gender of individuals based on their professional names.

## 4 Gold Gender Bias Test Dataset Preparation

### 4.1 Dataset Collection and Composition

The gold gender bias test dataset was crafted by combining sentences from public repositories (Sharma et al., 2022), with a thorough examination of gender biases across these selected target languages. We first collected an English-centric dataset from a variety of publicly available sources such as SimpleGEN, [5] and winomt,[6] focusing on relevance and diversity. To maintain balance, for every gender-specific sentence, we ensured there was an equivalent counterpart. For example, if a sentence says, "He is a doctor," a corresponding sentence like "She is a doctor" is included for gender parity.

[4]It should be translated in this context as "**ረድታዋለች**" (redtawalech) or "**ረድታቸዋለች**" (redtachewalech) for respect (she helped him) instead of "**ረድታለች**" (redtalech).

[5]SimpleGEN:https://github.com/arendu-zz/SimpleGEN

[6]winomt: https://github.com/manandey/bias_machine_translation/tree/main/data/base/winomt

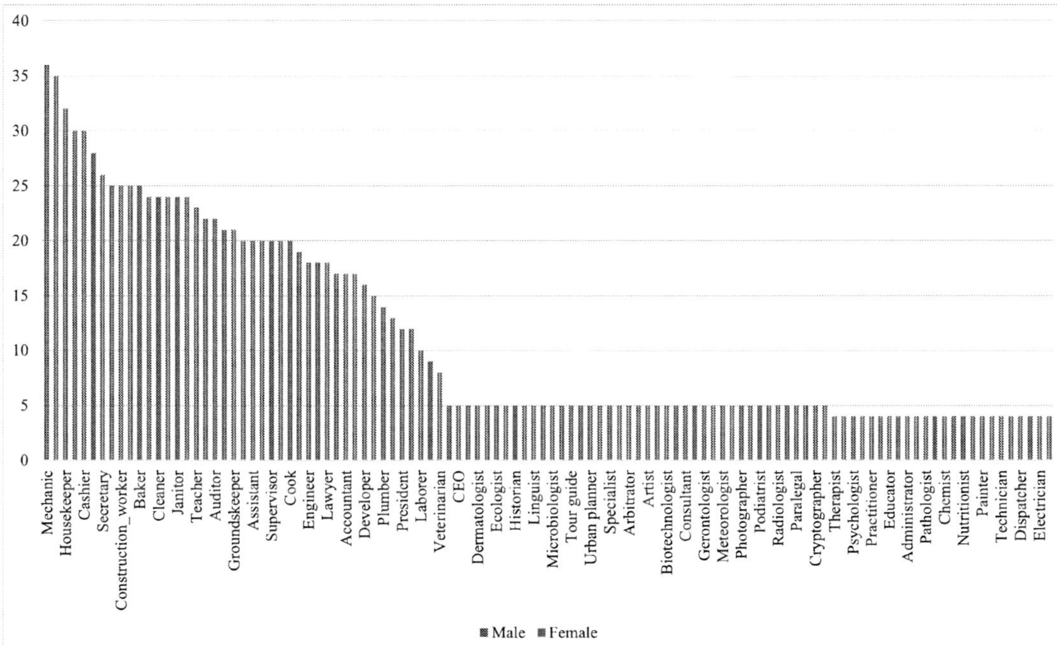


Figure 3: An example from our test dataset used out of 108 professional names.

However, these open-source datasets do not contain all professional names relevant to our communities of interest, even though they contain enough test datasets. For this reason, we used a crowdsourcing approach to collect additional data that reflects various professions. For this approach, we first incorporated the major professional names from (1) the Ethiopian Civil Service Commission list of job titles and (2) querying GPT 3.5 for recent technological professional words. Through this process, we collected 108 unique professional names. Figure 3 demonstrates a sample gender-balanced dataset of each professional name.

Then, we used paid freelancers for crowdsourcing and prepared a Google form containing clear and short instructions about the task. The goal of the crowdsourcing task was to create gender-balanced translation pairs from English-centric data from various sources. One of the key considerations was to include both pronouns and occupations in the dataset. This ensured that each profession is associated with different pronouns, such as "he," "his," and "him" for the masculine, and "she" and "her" for the feminine gender. For this task, ten freelancers were involved and signed an incentive agreement first. Then, we collected the English dataset from SimpleGEN (n=130), winomt (n=192), and crowd-sourced (n=2078), a total of 2400 sentences.

## 4.2 Dataset Translation

The next task is to translate this collected dataset into three Ethiopian languages: Amharic, Afaan Oromoo, and Tigrinya. Likewise, we have used paid linguistic experts who were proficient in one of our target languages, then undertook the translation process to preserve linguistic accuracy and capture cultural differences specific to each target language.

To prevent boredom and errors, we engaged six language experts and fluent speakers per language pair, totaling eighteen individuals from various universities. We assigned 600 sentence pairs per individual to keep the task manageable. After the translation, we recruited two paid professional linguists and editors for each language pair for quality checking.

The dataset used in this research, referred to as the Gold Gender Bias Test Dataset (GG-BTD), comprises 2400 sentence pairs for each language pair, specifically English-Amharic, English-Afaan Oromoo, and English-Tigrinya, resulting in a total of 7200 sentence pairs.

Within each language pair, the dataset maintains a comprehensive gender balance. Specifically, for each language pair, 1200 sentences represent masculine gender expressions, while the remaining 1200 sentences capture feminine gender expressions.

## 5 Evaluation Techniques

### 5.1 Automatic Evaluation

Different evaluation metrics are usually employed to automatically evaluate MT systems. These metrics are often based on word overlap and/or context similarity between references and model outputs. In our work, we employ both types of metrics to evaluate the quality of NLLB and Google MT that we consider in our study. Namely, we used SacreBleu (Post, 2018) and Chrf++ (Popović, 2017) machine translation evaluation metrics. We chose these MT evaluation metrics for several reasons. Firstly, these metrics are widely recognized and utilized in the field of MT research, ensuring compatibility and comparability with existing literature (Kadaoui et al., 2023).

Additionally, SacreBleu and Chrf++ are known for their robustness and effectiveness (Puduppully et al., 2023) in assessing translation quality across different languages and translation systems. Their ability to capture detailed aspects of translation quality, such as fluency, adequacy, and fidelity to the source text, makes them suitable choices for our evaluation framework. Furthermore, both metrics are supported by well-established methodologies and have demonstrated consistent performance in benchmarking studies, giving us confidence in their reliability. However, these metrics evaluate only the overall translation accuracy.

### 5.2 Human Evaluation

In this work, we relied solely on human-level evaluation techniques for evaluating gender bias. We assessed the gender bias in two MT systems: (1) open source NLLB model and (2) commercially available Google Translate. We chose these models since they support all three languages (Amharic, Tigrinya, Afaan Oromoo).

Given the high cost of human-level evaluation, we only evaluated the gender bias of Google Translate. For the human-level evaluation, first, we developed the evaluation guidelines shown in the appendix 10.1, and used the Potato annotation tool (Pei et al., 2022). Figure 4 shows the Potato annotation tool GUI for human-label evaluation, which supports all modern browsers and can be accessed both from computers and mobile phones for manual annotation. Criteria included gender biases, translation quality, and the accuracy of professional name translations. For evaluation, eighteen paid linguistic experts per language were selected. To avoid subjectivity, we divided evaluators into three groups and made the evaluation into three phases; this implies each sentence is evaluated three times. This is good for taking the majority vote for result analysis.

After each sentence in each of the three languages is evaluated by three evaluators, the annotation tool decides whether the sentence is biased or not by taking the majority vote of the three evaluators.

## 6 Result and Analysis

Figure 5 provides a clear comparison of responses across three language categories, allowing for insights into the distribution of responses within each language. It presents the gender bias across various language groups, delineating respondents' perceptions regarding the presence or absence of gender bias within each language category.

The data in Table 1 underscores the disparate perceptions of gender bias among respondents across different linguistic backgrounds. Particularly notable is the significantly higher percentage (92.96%) of Afaan Oromoo respondents who indicated observing gender bias compared to other language groups, with only 7.04% indicating otherwise. Similarly, in the Amharic group, approximately 72.50% of respondents indicated observing gender bias, contrasting with 27.50% who did not. Likewise, in the Tigrinya group, the majority (80.96%) indicated observing gender bias, while 19.04% expressed no bias. These findings reveal distinct patterns regarding whether speakers observe gender bias across language groups, suggesting potential implications for addressing and understanding

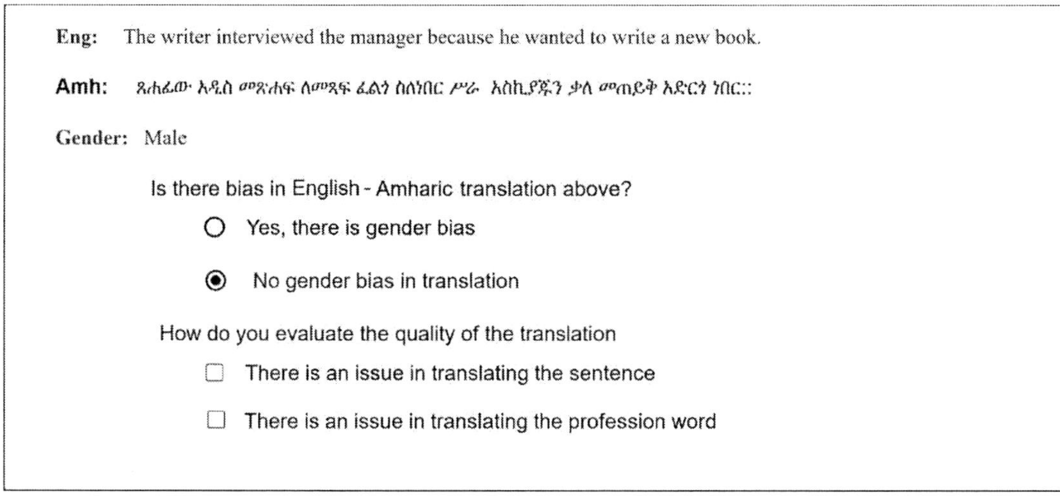


Figure 4: The Potato annotation GUI for the evaluation annotation.

Table 1: Translation Issues by Language

| | Amharic | Tigrinya | Afaan Oromoo |
|---|---|---|---|
| There is an issue in translating the sentence | 1429 | 936 | 918 |
| There is an issue in translating the profession | 258 | 475 | 612 |
| No issue | 510 | 619 | 421 |
| Both issues | 203 | 370 | 449 |
| Total | 2400 | 2400 | 2400 |

gender bias in MT within these communities.

Table 1 outlines translation issues across languages, categorized into "Translating the sentence issue" and "Professional word translation issue." Amharic records the highest instances of sentence translation issues at 1429, followed by Tigrinya with 936, and Afaan Oromoo with 918. Regarding professional word translation, Afaan Oromoo leads with 612 instances, trailed by Tigrinya at 475, and Amharic at 258. Tigrinya exhibits the fewest reported issues overall, with 619 sentences indicating no translation issues, compared to 510 for Amharic and 421 for Afaan Oromoo. Conversely, Amharic shows the highest incidence of respondents facing both types of issues at 203, followed by Afaan Oromoo at 449, and Tigrinya at 370. This data underscores the diverse challenges faced in translation across languages and provides valuable insights for enhancing translation quality and addressing language-specific obstacles.

Table 2 presents the evaluation results for NLLB and Google Translate models in the selected language pairs. The table is divided into rows representing different language pairs and columns representing the specific evaluation metrics. Each language pair is evaluated in both translation directions (e.g., Eng-Amh and Amh-Eng), providing insights into machine translation systems' translation quality and performance across various linguistic contexts.

The result shows that the Google MT system outperformed the NLLB model when using English as the source language in both evaluation metrics. This shows that translating English sentences into the target Ethiopian language is challenging for the model. On the other hand, the Google MT system showed better results compared to the NLLB model when translating English sentences into target Ethiopian languages. We observed better performance results when using English as the target language than when using it as the source language in the NLLB model. From this, we can see that for low-resource languages, publicly available MT models like NLLB are strug-

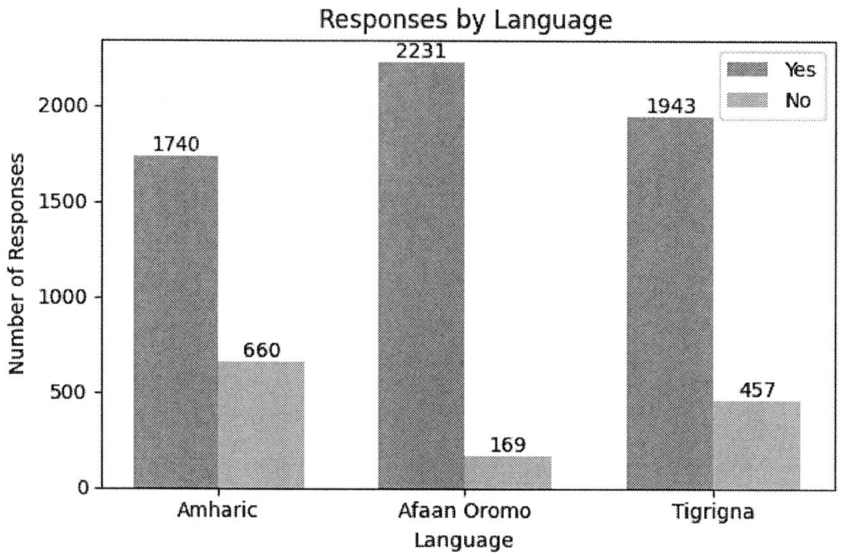


Figure 5: Illustration of the Google Translation Gender Bias test dataset human evaluation result. "Yes" and "No" are the answers to the question, "Is there bias in the translation?". "Yes" means the sentence contains gender bias when translated to a specified language. "No" is no gender bias observed in the translated sentence; the sentence is correctly translated.

Table 2: Automatic Evaluation Results

| Language | NLLB | | Google MT | |
|---|---|---|---|---|
| | SacreBleu ↑ | Chrf++ ↑ | SacreBleu ↑ | Chrf++ ↑ |
| Eng- Amh | 3.48 | 23.73 | 16.13 | 47.97 |
| Amh- Eng | 21.87 | 50.76 | - | |
| Eng- Orm | 4.85 | 34.85 | 22.96 | 56.71 |
| Orm- Eng | 17.80 | 41.63 | - | |
| Eng- Tir | 3.89 | 18.52 | 16.00 | 38.00 |
| Tir- Eng | 20.01 | 43.91 | - | |

gling to predict the correct translation when using English as the source language.

## 7 Conclusion and Future Work

In this paper, we curated a benchmark dataset for evaluating gender bias in machine translation systems in three low-resource languages. With this test dataset, we conducted a human-level gender bias evaluation of Google Translate and NLLB MT models for the given language pairs. The evaluation result shows that 92.96% of Eng-Orm, 80.96% of Eng-Tir, and 72.50% of Eng-Amh language pairs translations have a gender bias. In addition, we used the automatic evaluation to measure the translation quality of the currently available translation tools that support Amharic, Tigrinya, and Afaan Oromoo languages.

Our findings highlight the need for further research and development efforts to mitigate gender bias and promote gender-inclusive language translation. We observed that this work can be scaled up and used as a benchmark for other low-resource languages. In future work, we will use automatic gender bias evaluation metrics in addition to human evaluation. In addition, we will prepare a gender-balanced dataset for the given language, and we will fine-tune the currently available MT tools.

## 8 Limitations

The cost and time constraints limit our work to only three language pairs. The sources of gender biases in NLP are different such as the nature of the language gender, unbalanced professional names in the dataset, and gender unbalanced pronouns in the dataset. This work only focuses on unbalanced professional names.

## 9 Acknowledgments

We thank GRAIN for funding this work. We also thank the linguistic experts who participated in the annotation and translation of the gender bias test dataset. We thank Hailay Teklehaymanot for his feedback on our manuscript. Finally, we thank the reviewers for their extremely helpful remarks and feedback.

## References

Alhafni, Bashar, Nizar Habash, and Houda Bouamor. 2022. The arabic parallel gender corpus 2.0: Extensions and analyses. In Proceedings of the International Conference on Language Resources and Evaluation (LREC 2022), Marseille, France.

Barocas, Solon, Kate Crawford, Aaron Shapiro, and Hanna Wallach. 2017. The problem with bias: Allocative versus representational harms in machine learning. In 9th Annual conference of the special interest group for computing, information and society.

Blodgett, Su Lin, Solon Barocas, Hal Daumé III, and Hanna Wallach. 2020a. Language (technology) is power: A critical survey of" bias" in nlp. arXiv preprint arXiv:2005.14050.

Blodgett, Su Lin, Solon Barocas, Hal Daumé Iii, and Hanna Wallach. 2020b. Language (Technology) is Power: A Critical Survey of "Bias" in NLP. ACL Anthology, pages 5454–5476, July.

Cho, Won Ik, Ji Won Kim, Seok Min Kim, and Nam Soo Kim. 2019. On measuring gender bias in translation of gender-neutral pronouns. arXiv preprint arXiv:1905.11684.

Crawford, Kate. 2017. The trouble with bias.

Habash, Nizar, Houda Bouamor, and Christine Chung. 2019. Automatic gender identification and reinflection in arabic. In Proceedings of the First Workshop on Gender Bias in Natural Language Processing, pages 155–165.

Kadaoui, Karima, Samar M Magdy, Abdul Waheed, Md Tawkat Islam Khondaker, Ahmed Oumar El-Shangiti, El Moatez Billah Nagoudi, and Muhammad Abdul-Mageed. 2023. Tarjamat: Evaluation of bard and chatgpt on machine translation of ten arabic varieties. arXiv preprint arXiv:2308.03051.

Pei, Jiaxin, Aparna Ananthasubramaniam, Xingyao Wang, Naitian Zhou, Apostolos Dedeloudis, Jackson Sargent, and David Jurgens. 2022. POTATO: The portable text annotation tool. In Che, Wanxiang and Ekaterina Shutova, editors, Proceedings of the 2022 Conference on Empirical Methods in Natural Language Processing: System Demonstrations, pages 327–337, Abu Dhabi, UAE, December. Association for Computational Linguistics.

Popović, Maja. 2017. chrf++: words helping character n-grams. In Proceedings of the second conference on machine translation, pages 612–618.

Post, Matt. 2018. A call for clarity in reporting bleu scores. arXiv preprint arXiv:1804.08771.

Prates, Marcelo OR, Pedro H Avelar, and Luís C Lamb. 2020. Assessing gender bias in machine translation: a case study with google translate. Neural Computing and Applications, 32:6363–6381.

Puduppully, Ratish, Raj Dabre, Ai Ti Aw, and Nancy F Chen. 2023. Decomposed prompting for machine translation between related languages using large language models. arXiv preprint arXiv:2305.13085.

Renduchintala, Adithya, Denise Díaz, Kenneth Heafield, Xian Li, and Mona Diab. 2021. Gender bias amplification during Speed-Quality optimization in Neural Machine Translation. ACL Anthology, pages 99–109, August.

Savoldi, Beatrice, Marco Gaido, Luisa Bentivogli, Matteo Negri, and Marco Turchi. 2021. Gender bias in machine translation. Transactions of the Association for Computational Linguistics, 9:845–874.

Sharma, Shanya, Manan Dey, and Koustuv Sinha. 2022. How sensitive are translation systems to extra contexts? mitigating gender bias in neural machine translation models through relevant contexts. In Findings of the Association for Computational Linguistics: EMNLP 2022, pages 1968–1984, Abu Dhabi, United Arab Emirates, Dec. Association for Computational Linguistics.

Stanovsky, Gabriel, Noah A Smith, and Luke Zettlemoyer. 2019. Evaluating gender bias in machine translation. arXiv preprint arXiv:1906.00591.

Talat, Zeerak, Aurelie Neveol, Stella Biderman, Miruna Clinciu, Manan Dey, Shayne Longpre, Sasha Luccioni, Maraim Masoud, Margaret Mitchell, Dragomir Radev, Shanya Sharma, Arjun Subramonian, Jaesung Tae, Samson Tan, Deepak Tunuguntla, and Oskar Van Der Wal. 2022. You reap what you sow: On the Challenges of Bias Evaluation Under Multilingual Settings. ACL Anthology, pages 26–41, May.

Team, NLLB, Marta R. Costa-Jussà, James Cross, Onur Çelebi, Maha Elbayad, Kenneth Heafield, Kevin Heffernan, Elahe Kalbassi, Janice Lam, Daniel Licht, Jean Maillard, Anna Sun, Skyler Wang, Guillaume Wenzek, Al Youngblood, Bapi Akula, Loïc Barrault, Gabriel Mejía González, Prangthip Hansanti, John Hoffman, Semarley Jarrett, Kaushik Ram Sadagopan, Dirk Rowe, Shannon Spruit, Chau Tran, Pierre Andrews, Necip Fazil Ayan, Shruti Bhosale, Sergey Edunov, Angela Fan, Cynthia Gao, Vedanuj Goswami, Francisco Guzmán, Philipp Koehn, Alexandre Mourachko, Christophe Ropers, Safiyyah Saleem, Holger Schwenk, and Jeff Wang. 2022. No language left behind: Scaling human-centered machine translation. arXiv preprint arXiv:2207.04672.

Wairagala, Eric Peter, Jonathan Mukiibi, Jeremy Francis Tusubira, Claire Babirye, Joyce Nakatumba-Nabende, Andrew Katumba, and Ivan Ssenkungu. 2022. Gender bias evaluation in luganda-english machine translation. In Proceedings of the 15th biennial conference of the Association for Machine Translation in the Americas (Volume 1: Research Track), pages 274–286.

## 10 Appendix

### 10.1 Appendix: Human-level Evaluation Guideline

Hello everyone,

We are excited to invite you to participate in an important evaluation task aimed at assessing gender bias in Google Translation from English into Amharic, Afaan Oromoo, and Tigrinya. As well as, to evaluate the quality of the overall translation, you are asked to evaluate the translation issue of the whole sentence and whether there is an issue with professional name translation only. As an evaluator, your valuable insights will help us ensure that translations accurately reflect gender inclusivity and professionalism. By carefully reviewing each sentence pair and considering both gender specification and professional terminology, you will play a pivotal role in enhancing translation quality. Your diligent efforts in evaluating 400 sentences will contribute to creating more inclusive and accurate translations. Thank you for your time and cooperation in this endeavor. Let's work together to promote fairness and accuracy in translation.

Evaluation Task: Gender Bias in Google Translation from English into Amharic, Afaan Oromoo, and Tigrinya

1. Login Credentials: Use the provided username and password to access the evaluation platform.

2. Accessing the Task: Open the designated link on your preferred device, whether mobile or computer.

3. Evaluation Procedure:

   - Reviewing Sentences: Carefully examine each provided sentence in English alongside its translation into Amharic, Afaan Oromoo, or Tigrinya.
   - Identifying Gender Bias: Determine the presence of gender bias by considering two factors:
     - Gender Section: Assess whether the translated gender (feminine or masculine) aligns with the gender specified in the original sentence.
     - Professional Words: Check if professional terms are translated with the same gender as provided in the original sentence.
   - Selecting Response: Choose "Yes, there is gender bias" if bias is detected, or "No, gender bias in translation" if not.
   - Evaluate the quality of translation: Select the first check box "There is an issue in translating the sentence" if there is an issue in overall translation or/and select the second check box "There is an issue in translating the profession word".
   - Moving to Next Sentence: Click the "Next" button after making your assessment to proceed to the next set of sentences.

4. Total Sentences: The evaluation task consists of 400 sentences to be assessed.

5. Completion and Compensation: Upon completing the evaluation of all 400 sentences, compensation will be provided according to the prearranged agreement.

We appreciate your dedication and cooperation in contributing to this evaluation task. Your feedback is crucial for improving translation quality and mitigating gender bias.

## 10.2 Appendix: List of Pronouns in English, Amharic, Tigrinya, Afaan Oromoo

Table 3: Pronouns in English, Amharic, Tigrinya, and Afaan Oromoo.
Key: M=Masculine, F=Feminine, sg=singular, pl=plural, R=Respect

| English | Amharic | Tigrinya | Afaan Oromoo |
|---|---|---|---|
| I | እኔ (əne) | ኣነ (anä) | ana, na |
| We | እኛ (əñña) | ንሕና (nəḥəna) | nu |
| You (M. sg.) | አንተ (antä) | ንስኻ (nəssəxa) | |
| You (F. sg.) | አንቺ (anči) | ንስኺ (nəssəxi) | |
| You (sg.) | | | si |
| You (R) | እርስዎ (ərswo) | | |
| You (F, R) | | ንሰን/ንስኸን (nsen/nskhn) | |
| You (M, R) | | ንሶም/ንስኹም (nsom/nskhum) | |
| You (pl.) | እናንተ (ənnantä) | | isin |
| You (M. pl.) | | ንስኻትኩም (nəssəxatkum) | |
| You (F. pl.) | | ንስኻትክን (nəssəxatkən) | |
| He | እሱ (əssu) | ንሱ (nəssu) | isa |
| She | እሷ (əsswa) | ንሳ (nəssa) | isii, ishii, isee, ishee |
| S/he (R) | እሳቸው (əssaččäw) | | |
| She (R) | | ንሰን (nsen) | |
| He (R) | | ንሶም (nsom) | |
| They | እነሱ (ənnässu) | | isaan |
| They (M.) | | ንሳቶም (nəssatom) | |
| They (F.) | | ንሳተን (nəssatän) | |

# Sparks of Fairness: Preliminary Evidence of Commercial Machine Translation as English-to-German Gender-Fair Dictionaries

**Manuel Lardelli♣, Timm Dill♢, Giuseppe Attanasio♠, Anne Lauscher♢**

♣ University of Graz, Austria
♢ University of Hamburg, Germany
♠ Instituto de Telecomunicações, Lisbon, Portugal
manuel.lardelli01@gmail.com

## Abstract

Bilingual dictionaries are bedrock components for several language tasks, including translation. However, dictionaries are traditionally fixed in time, thus excluding those neologisms and neo-morphemes that challenge the language's nominal morphology. The need for a more dynamic, mutable alternative makes Machine Translation (MT) systems become an extremely valuable avenue. This paper investigates whether commercial MT can be used as bilingual dictionaries for gender-fair translation. We focus on the English-to-German pair, where notional gender in the source requires gender inflection in the target. We translated a dataset with person-referring terms using Google Translate, Microsoft Bing, and DeepL and discovered that while each system is heavily biased towards the masculine gender, DeepL often provides gender-fair alternatives to users, especially with plurals.

## 1 Introduction

*"The past is print dictionaries; the present is print dictionaries with some electronic versions of the same text; the future must be print dictionaries and truly electronic dictionaries, compiled afresh for the new medium, enriched with new types of information the better to meet the needs of the multifarious users."*

– *Beryl Sinclair, 1996*

The way we speak about humans influences our mental representation of them – psychological research shows that thus, using *gender-fair language* can reduce gender-related stereotyping and discrimination (Sczesny et al., 2016). Accordingly, many national and international organizations in Europe and beyond (e.g., universities and even the European Parliament[1]) are increasingly adopting gender-fair language, and, for instance, publishing guidelines and recommendations on the topic. In translation, the topic of gender-fair language (GFL) is specifically interesting as we are often facing a gender-neutral person word (e.g., *the workers* in English), which needs to be translated to a language like German, in which using a gendered form would be the most traditional choice (e.g., *die Arbeiter* or *die Arbeiterinnen* in German). Often, using a gendered form only will, however, simply reflect existing stereotypes (e.g., occupational stereotypes) and also lead to the reinforced exclusion of individuals who do not identify with the specific grammatical gender chosen, like non-binary individuals (Dev et al., 2021).

In this work, we hypothesize that, given the widespread use of language technology, Machine Translation (MT) can be a key enabler in the adoption of gender-fair language for non-native speakers and in scenarios involving organizations that act internationally. Still, the existing research landscape on the behavior of commercial MT systems concerning gender-fair language is scarce: existing studies have looked at a few specific language pairs (and translation directions) scenarios, and domains only (e.g., (Savoldi et al., 2023), *inter alia*). For instance, there exists barely information on gender fairness in English-to-German MT. As MT systems are increasingly used as vocabularies



[1] https://www.europarl.europa.eu/cmsdata/151780/GNL_Guidelines_EN.pdf



*Proceedings of the 2nd International Workshop on Gender-Inclusive Translation Technologies*, pages 12–21
June 27, 2024 ©2024 European Association for Machine Translation

(Cotelli Kureth et al., 2023) (i.e., to translate single words without any further context), we pose the following research question: ***Can commercial MT be used as English-to-German gender-fair dictionaries?*** If we would find commercial MT to produce gender-fair translations, one could think of leveraging this potential for bootstrapping more research on gender-fair MT, further motivating our question.

**Contributions.** We present the first study on English-to-German gender-fair language in commercial MT focused on dictionary-like translations to date. To this end, we employ a community-created gender-fair dictionary for German, from which we sample seed nouns, which we translate into English. We then start from the English terms, and (**1**) conduct a pre-study in which we assess the general potential of three popular commercial MT systems (Google Translate, Microsoft Bing, and DeepL) for gender-fair MT. Based on these findings, we (**2**) conduct an in-depth study on DeepL, in which we test singular and plural forms and provide statistics on the exact type of gender-fair language we observe. Our findings show, for instance, that DeepL often provides gender-fair alternatives to the users, but that the system is heavily biased towards masculine translations (roughly 67% of the outputs). Interestingly, in the plural, gender-fair outputs are much more frequent than in the singular, with the participial form and BinnenI being the most common. We hope that our work fuels more research on gender-fair language in English-to-German MT.

**Bias Statement.** We collect English-to-German system outputs and analyze the overt gender of the translations. If a gender-fair output is present, we categorize it into its specific form. Our work therefore addresses overt gender bias in the output, and, accordingly, the issue of ***representational harm*** **(stereotyping and exclusion)** (Barocas et al., 2017).

## 2 Related Work

Bilingual dictionaries are bedrocks of various linguistic applications, including language learning (Thompson, 1987) and translation. Motivated by such an important role, several efforts have studied how to extract them at scale (Nagata et al., 2001) or integrate them in neural machine translation systems (Duan et al., 2020; Zhang et al., 2021). In this paper, we study modern commercial translation systems' as EN-DE bilingual dictionaries with a focused eye on gender-fair forms.

Our work is part of a broader discourse on fairness and inclusivity in machine translation. Neural and commercial systems are known to encode stereotypical views on genders (Savoldi et al., 2021), leading to brittle gender inflection capabilities in grammatical gender languages (Stanovsky et al., 2019; Attanasio et al., 2023), covert biases in genderless languages (Ciora et al., 2021), and inadequate handling of neo-morphemes (Lauscher et al., 2023) and named entities (Saunders and Olsen, 2023). Further, systems are nearly incapable of gender-neutral translation for human entity nouns in EN-IT (Piergentili et al., 2023) and DE-EN (Savoldi et al., 2023). To ground automatic translation with human practices, recent studies have reported on neutralization and gender-inclusive strategies used by professional translators (Daems, 2023; Paolucci et al., 2023) and MT post-editors (Lardelli and Gromann, 2023a).

These findings and research efforts underscore the need for our research on commercial MT dictionary capabilities. As Sinclair poses it, static, bilingual dictionaries suffer from gaps in coverage, e.g., failing to include neologisms (Atkins, 1996). This work studies whether modern commercial systems have fixed on traditional gender forms or are indeed "meeting the needs of the multifarious user."

## 3 Background

As a basis for this work, we first introduce the relationship between gender and language (§3.1), followed by the definition of gender-fair language (GFL) (§3.2), and possible strategies in German (§3.3).

### 3.1 Linguistic Gender

The term gender may refer to a linguistic feature and an extra-linguistic reality. Linguistic gender can be divided into grammatical, lexical, and referential (Cao and Daumé III, 2020; Corbett, 1991). Grammatical gender pertains to the classification of nouns into categories such as masculine, feminine, and neuter. For instance, "sun" is masculine in Italian ("il sole") but feminine in German ("die Sonne"). Lexical gender describes the semantic property of femaleness or maleness of a noun, such as "mother" and "father". Referential gender refers to the extra-linguistic reality, i.e., the gender of a noun reflects the gender identity of the referent, e.g., "Schauspieler" (EN: male actor) and "Schauspielerin (EN: female actor) in German.

Based on linguistic gender, languages can be classified into grammatical gender, notional gender, and genderless languages (Stahlberg et al., 2007; McConnell-Ginet, 2013). The first, e.g., German, have grammatical, lexical, and referential gender. Consequently, they are highly inflected and mark gender very often. The second, e.g., English, usually have lexical and referential gender. Therefore, they are sometimes marked for gender. Genderless languages, e.g., Turkish, have only lexical gender and rarely carry gender inflection.

### 3.2 Gender-Fair Language

A common linguistic phenomenon in grammatical and notional gender languages is the masculine generic, i.e., the use of masculine forms to refer to both men and people in general. This specific language practice has drawn the attention of feminists who, in the field of linguistics and translation studies amongst others, have analysed how patriarchal language is used to oppress women and consequently advocated for GFL (Simon, 1996; Kramer, 2016).

As in Sczesny et al. (2016), we use "gender-fair" to subsume both gender-neutral and gender-inclusive approaches. The former avoid gender marking by using passive constructions, indefinite pronouns, and gender-neutral nouns. The latter make all genders visible through typographical characters (e.g., gender star (*) in German), symbols (e.g., schwa (ə) in Italian), and neomorphemes (e.g., "e" in Spanish).

Furthermore, the relationship between linguistic gender and gender identity is not one-to-one (Cao and Daumé III, 2020). In many European languages, only the masculine and feminine gender are used in reference to people (Deutscher, 2010). Therefore, non-binary representation requires breaking traditional grammar rules and new GFL strategies have been proposed in the last few years (Lardelli and Gromann, 2023b; López, 2019).

### 3.3 Gender-Fair German

Lardelli and Gromann (2023b) provide an overview of GFL strategies in German, which we summarise here due to space constraints. The researchers identify four main approaches:

1. Gender-Neutral Rewording: strategies to avoid gender marking, e.g., the use of participial forms, passive constructions, and gender-neutral terms.

2. Gender-Inclusive Characters: e.g., gender star (*) is used to separate masculine and feminine forms of words as in *"der*die Autor*in"* (EN: the author), usually to avoid masculine generics.

3. Gender-Neutral Characters: e.g., "x" is used to replace gender suffixes (e.g., *"dix Autorx"*) in contexts where gender is unknown or irrelevant to the context of the conversation.

4. Gender-Fair Neosystems: for instance, "ens" is used as a morpheme to create new articles (e.g., *"dens"*), pronouns (e.g., *"dens"*), and nouns (e.g. *"Authorens"*). These strategies are usually devised by non-binary people as a means to be included in language.

## 4 Method

The proposed method is inspired by research on gender bias in MT (Savoldi et al., 2021), combining the creation of a dataset – containing common nouns referring to people –, its automatic translation with three commercial MT systems (DeepL[2], Google Translate[3], and Microsoft Bing[4]), and their output analysis.

Since there is currently no standard for GFL and, as found in studies on translation and post-editing (Lardelli and Gromann, 2023a; Lardelli, 2023), its implementation varies greatly. Therefore, we started from the *"Genderwörterbuch"*[5]. This is a community-created German vocabulary where users add gender-fair, usually neutral, alternatives to terms commonly marked for gender. The terms contained in the vocabulary are usually nouns referring to people, but the resource also contains expressions with pronouns (e.g. *"der eine oder der andere"*, EN: "one or the other") and short phrases (e.g. *"Das Angebot richtet sich an Anfänger und Fortgeschrittene"*, EN: "the offer is aimed at beginners and advanced students"). We focused on nouns referring to people and used the vocabulary to select suitable terms for our study.

[2]https://www.deepl.com/translator
[3]https://translate.google.com
[4]https://www.bing.com/translator
[5]https://geschicktgendern.de/

We first randomly selected 128 lemmas. We filtered out those that are already neutral, e.g., *"Star"*, whose grammatical gender is masculine, but it is used for all genders and has no other inflected variants. We also removed polysemous terms, e.g., *"aid"*, to facilitate translation into English. The final size of our datasets is 115 lemmas.

After translating each of the sampled lemmas into English, one of the authors also enriched the dataset with the English plural form. An extract from our dataset is shown in Table 1. To date, most research on gender bias in MT focuses on the translation of professions only (Prates et al., 2020). Conversely, our dataset includes common nouns too (e.g., *"donor"*).

| German Lemma | English Singular | English Plural |
|---|---|---|
| der Leser | the reader | the readers |
| der Berater | the counsellor | the counsellors |

**Table 1:** Examples for entries in our dataset

MT systems are increasingly used as bilingual dictionaries (Cotelli Kureth et al., 2023). We were interested in widely used commercial MT systems, such as DeepL, Google Translate, and Microsoft Bing, as possible English-to-German gender-fair dictionaries. Although to a different extent, these tools offer dictionary functions and/or propose some alternatives for each translation. Therefore, between December 2023 and April 2024, we back-translated the English terms included in our dataset into German, both in the singular and plural, via the User Interface (UI) of each of the selected MT systems.

First, we conducted an exploratory study by translating the first 20 terms in our dataset. For each English term, we pasted the translations along with all the alternatives proposed by the MT systems into an Excel sheet. We initially translated terms along with the definite article. This is important because in German some nouns have only a gender form but require masculine or feminine articles, e.g. *"der/die Bedienstete"* (EN: "the employee"). However, we noted that Google Translate and Microsoft Bing provide only one translation when doing so. Therefore, for these two systems, we re-translated the terms by omitting the definite article.

We discarded Google Translate and Microsoft Bing based on the initial findings (§5.1): the alternative translations proposed by both systems are usually in the masculine form. Conversely, DeepL's outputs contain gender-fair alternatives considerably more often. Hence, we translated the whole dataset only with DeepL. One of the authors – an expert in GFL and translation – evaluated the translations. In the first step, a quantitative analysis was conducted: the author annotated the overt gender of the translation, i.e., masculine (M), feminine (F), gender-inclusive (GI), and gender-neutral (GN). Wrong translations (W) were also annotated. In Table 2, an example of the annotation for the translations of the English term "the colleagues" is reported. In this context, wrong refers to semantics (i.e., the German term has a different meaning than the English source), and grammar (e.g., wrong number or no agreement between article and noun). In the second step, the focus was on the type of gender-fair language strategy used by the system. Finally, another author whose first language is German replicated the analysis in order to validate the results. The percentage agreement between the two raters was calculated. Differences in the annotation were discussed to reach a consensus.

## 5 Results

First, we summarise the results of the exploratory study (§5.1), then we provide an overview of the results obtained with DeepL and focus on the overt gender of the machine-translated outputs in German (§5.2). We subsequently analyze which gender-fair, i.e., inclusive and neutral, strategies are found in the singular (§5.2.1) and plural (§5.2.2).

### 5.1 Findings from the Exploratory Study

Table 3 presents an overview of the results of the exploratory study with Google Translate (GT), Microsoft Bing (MB), and DeepL. The table focuses on the overt gender of the machine translations for the first twenty seed words in our dataset: M indicates masculine, G feminine, GI gender-inclusive, GN gender-neutral, W wrong translation, T the sum of all translations including the alternatives proposed by the MT systems.

First, when translating single nouns without an article, both Google Translate and Microsoft Bing usually, but not always, provide gender-specific translations for the masculine and the feminine (Kuczmarski, 2018; Translator, 2023). This feature, however, does not seem to be available for

| Source Term | Translations | Overt Gender | | | | | GFL Strategy |
|---|---|---|---|---|---|---|---|
| | | M | F | GI | GN | W | |
| The colleagues | Die Kollegen | x | | | | | |
| | Die Kolleginnen und Kollegen | | | x | | | double form |
| | Die Mitarbeiter | x | | | | | |
| | Die Kollegen und Kolleginnen | | | x | | | double form |

**Table 2:** Annotation example for the German translations of "the colleagues"

| | | M | F | GI | GN | W | T |
|---|---|---|---|---|---|---|---|
| **GT** | Singular | 32 | 13 | 0 | 2 | 5 | 52 |
| | Plural | 19 | 6 | 0 | 1 | 0 | 26 |
| **MB** | Singular | 25 | 1 | 0 | 3 | 3 | 32 |
| | Plural | 29 | 0 | 2 | 6 | 0 | 37 |
| **DeepL** | Singular | 49 | 17 | 2 | 1 | 7 | 76 |
| | Plural | 43 | 2 | 14 | 9 | 4 | 72 |

**Table 3:** Results from the exploratory study: overt gender of the machine translations in the singular and plural

the German language in Bing Translator and it is not available at all in DeepL.

Second, we noted that all systems are systematically biased towards the masculine forms, which represent more than half of all translations. While all systems also provide possible alternative translations, Google Translate and Microsoft Bing generally default to the masculine. For instance, the first system outputs *"Siedler"* (EN: settler, masculine) and *"Siedlerin"* (EN: settler, feminine) as a gender-specific translation for the English noun "settler" but it also suggests two synonyms in the masculine form, i.e., *"der Ansiedler"* and *"der Kolonist"*. Both gender-inclusive (0-2%) and gender-neutral (1-6%) are rare in Google Translate's and Microsoft Bings's outputs and occur more often in DeepL, i.e. up to respectively 14% and 9% in the plural.

Finally, the number of alternative translations provided by Google Translate considerably decreases in the plural. DeepL is the system that provides the highest amount of alternatives, e.g. 76 translations against 52 (Google Translate) and 32 (Microsoft Bing) in the singular. Based on these preliminary findings, we decided to continue the study by translating our entire dataset with DeepL only.

### 5.2 General Findings with DeepL

Table 4 summarises the results for the translation of both singular and plural words contained in our dataset. The table focuses on the overt gender of the DeepL outputs. Note that the total of translations does not amount to 115 because we analysed all alternatives suggested by the system.

| | | M | F | GI | GN | W |
|---|---|---|---|---|---|---|
| Singular | *N* | 285 | 79 | 6 | 17 | 44 |
| | % | 66 | 18 | 1 | 4 | 10 |
| Plural | *N* | 279 | 9 | 45 | 62 | 20 |
| | % | 67 | 2 | 11 | 15 | 5 |

**Table 4:** Translation results with DeepL: overt gender of the singular and plural terms

The percentage agreement between the two raters was 96% in the overt gender annotation. The differences were discussed. In most cases, one of the two raters made a mistake in the gender annotation. For instance, the English term "mountaineer" was translated amongst others as "Bergbewohner", which indicates a person who lives in a mountain area. The second rater annotated this alternative as semantically wrong, which is not. An interesting source of disagreement in the annotation was the use of neutral forms in the plural. For example, the term "prosecutors" was translated as "Staatsanwaltschaft" and its plural form "Staatsanwaltschaften" was suggested as well (EN: " office(s) of the Public Prosecutor). One rater considered "Staatsanwaltschaft" as a wrong translation. However, the term is a collective noun and it could therefore be argued that it may be used for one or more referents, in this case one or more prosecutor(s). It is not always possible or desirable to decide if the translation of a single term is correct without analysing its use in a broader context, which represents a limitation of the present study (see §6) and, more generally, of the use of MT systems as dictionaries.

DeepL is strongly biased towards the masculine gender, which appears in about 67% of the translations both in the plural and in the singular. Feminine translations occur less frequently, i.e., in 18% of the outputs for the singular. This value drops to 2% in the plural. The number of gender-inclusive and neutral forms is very low in the singular, 1% and 4% respectively. This value, however, considerably increases in the plural to 11% and 15%. Since words in isolation were translated and DeepL lacked contextual information for the selection of an appropriate term, semantically and/or grammatically wrong translations make up 10% and 5% of the outputs respectively, e.g., *"Depotbank"* (EN: "custodian bank") as a translation for the person term "custodian".

#### 5.2.1 Gender-Fair Forms in the Singular

In the singular, two gender-inclusive strategies were found, as shown in Table 5. The first is the use of masculine and feminine forms separated by a slash, e.g., *"der Sportler/die Sportlerin"* (EN:"sportsperson"), which occurred four times in the translated dataset. The second is using a slash to combine the masculine and feminine definite article and a participial form for the noun, e.g., *"die/der Vorsitzende"* (EN: "the chairperson"), which occurred twice. Note that these approaches are not inclusive of non-binary people: the use of gender star, e.g. *"der*die Sportler*in"* and *"der*die Vorsitzende"*, would be the most common gender-fair alternative nowadays to indicate that there are more than two genders.

| **Gender-Inclusive** | *N* |
|---|---|
| masculine/feminine | 4 |
| article with / + participial form | 2 |

**Table 5:** Gender-inclusive forms in the singular

Gender-neutral forms were slightly more frequent and three main strategies were found, as shown in Table 6. The first was the use of abstract, usually collective, nouns, e.g., *"die Projektleitung"* (EN: "the project leadership" instead of "the project leader"), which occurred nine times. The second was the use of a noun that is already gender-neutral, e.g., *"der Neuling"* (EN: "the beginner"), which occurred four times. In these cases, the German term has the masculine grammatical gender, but it is commonly used for all genders. The third strategy found in the translation outputs was the use of the term *"Person"* (EN: "person") or *"Mensch"* (EN: "human") to build gender-neutral compounds, e.g., *"die Geschäftsperson"* (EN: "the businessperson"). This strategy too occurred four times.

| **Gender-Neutral** | *N* |
|---|---|
| Abstract Nouns | 9 |
| Neutral Nouns | 4 |
| Expressions with Person | 4 |

**Table 6:** Gender-neutral forms in the singular

#### 5.2.2 Gender-Fair Forms in the Plural

Gender-fair outputs were more frequent in the plural. Three gender-inclusive strategies were found. The first was the BinnenI, e.g., *"die MinisterInnen"* (EN: the ministers), and occurred twenty-two times in the translated dataset. The BinnenI is similar to gender-inclusive characters, such as gender star (*), which are now more common in German (Körner et al., 2022). The second strategy was the use of double forms, i.e., the masculine and feminine gender are mentioned as in *"Die Koordinatorinnen und Koordinatoren"* (EN: the coordinators). It occurred twenty times in the translations. The last gender-inclusive strategy is the use of a slash (/) as an inclusive character, e.g., *"die Blogger/innen"* (EN: the bloggers).

| **Gender-Inclusive** | *N* |
|---|---|
| BinnenI | 22 |
| Double Forms | 19 |
| Slash | 4 |

**Table 7:** Gender-inclusive forms in the plural

As concerns gender-neutral language, the same strategies as in (§5.2.1) were found with the addition of participial forms, which were the most frequent with twenty-two occurrences. German verbs can be nominalized by using participial forms, e.g., *"die Abgefraten"* (EN: "the respondents") as found in the analysed translations. While the articles and/or the noun declension is gender-specific in the singular, participial forms are gender-neutral in the plural – hence, they are a quite common strategy to avoid the generic masculine.

| **Gender-Neutral** | *N* |
|---|---|
| Participial Forms | 22 |
| Abstract Nouns | 20 |
| Compounds with People | 11 |
| Neutral Nouns | 7 |

**Table 8:** Gender-neutral forms in the plural

Abstract nouns occurred frequently too, i.e., twenty times. For instance, "the prosecutors" was translated into *"die Staatsanwaltschaft"* which, back-translated into English, indicates the office of the Public Prosecutor. Expressions with the term *"Leute"* (EN: people) were found eleven times in the translated dataset, e.g., *"die Bauleute"* for "the builders". Finally, neutral nouns were the least common gender-neutral strategy with seven occurrences, e.g., *"Die Grundschulkinder"* for "the primary school pupils".

## 6 Discussion

In the present contribution, we were interested in using three commercial MT models as English-to-German gender-fair dictionaries. Unsurprisingly, the results suggest that commercial MT models are still systematically biased towards masculine forms when translating from a notional gender, English, into a grammatical gender language, German.

In our exploratory study, we find that Google Translate usually generates gender-specific translations, but only in the masculine and feminine genders. This feature is not available in Microsoft Bing and DeepL. Both Google Translate and Microsoft Bing provide alternative translations, usually synonyms, in their dictionary interface. These alternatives are, however, generally masculine. Conversely, DeepL offers numerous alternatives that are also gender-fair.

The main study confirms that DeepL is heavily biased towards the masculine with about 67% of outputs having this overt gender both in the singular and plural. A great difference emerges between singular and plural: the number of feminine translations significantly decreases from 18% to 2%. Conversely, the number of gender-inclusive and neutral translations increases from 1% to 11% and 4% to 15% respectively. There are at least two main reasons for this phenomenon.

First, some nouns are gender-specific in the singular form, but not in the plural. For instance, the term "traveller" has different declensions. Without articles, the masculine form is *"Reisender"* whilst the feminine is *"Reisende"*. In the plural, there is one form only, i.e., *"Reisende"*. Second, German-speaking countries have a relatively strong feminist tradition and gender-fair language policies to avoid masculine generics were introduced several years ago (Sczesny et al., 2016). GFL is now quite common in, e.g., administrative texts where different gender-fair strategies, such as participial forms and gender star (*), are increasingly used for the declension of plural terms (Körner et al., 2022).

In the translations generated by DeepL, several gender-neutral and inclusive forms were found. Gender-neutral forms included compounds with neutral terms such as person (e.g. *"der spekulative Mensch"*, the speculating person), abstract nouns (e.g., *"die Staatsanwaltschaft"*, the prosecutor's office), and participial forms (e.g. *"die Vorsitzenden"*, the presidents). Gender-inclusive forms were also found, including BinnenI (e.g. *"die KoordinatorInnen"*, the coordinators), slash (e.g. *"die Mitbürger/innen"*, the fellow citizens), and double forms (e.g. *"die Betreuerinnen und Betreuer"*, the counsellors).

Though DeepL seems to be receptive of gender-fair forms that, probably quite rarely, occur in the training data, gender-inclusive strategies found in the outputs are usually outdated mostly because they are considered inclusive of binary genders only. For instance, BinnenI was once commonly used and studies about its effect on mental representations date back more than twenty years ago (Stahlberg and Sczesny, 2001). This strategy has nowadays been replaced by the use of gender-inclusive characters such as gender star (*) (Körner et al., 2022).

The findings of this study show how current commercial MT systems cannot keep up with linguistic change. The field of gender-fair language is constantly evolving and there is yet no one-size-fits-all solution to issues of gender representation (Gromann et al., 2023). In fact, the selection of a gender-fair language strategy is highly context-dependent (Lardelli and Gromann, 2023a; Gromann et al., 2023; Lardelli, 2023). For this reason, future research endeavours on MT debiasing should be the result of interdisciplinary efforts, involving computational linguistics, sociolinguistics, and translation studies amongst others.

To conclude, we discuss three major limitations of the present study. The first concerns the non-replicability of the results. Unfortunately, we don't have insights into the system used by Google, DeepL, and Microsoft Bing. Updates and/or re-training may lead to changes in the outputs over time. The second involves the analysis of gender-neutral and inclusive strategies. As already explained, there is no standard for GFL and creativity is often required. The soundness of gender-fair solutions might hence be judged differently among experts and, more importantly, depends on the broader context, i.e. at least the text, in which such solutions are used. Finally, we considered one language pair only because of the high amount of manual work involved in the translation of our dataset and its analysis.

## 7 Conclusion

In this study on gender bias in MT, we investigated the use of three commercial systems as English-to-German gender-fair dictionaries. Drawing on a community-created gender-fair dictionary, we developed a dataset including 115 gender-specific terms for which gender-fair alternatives in German were proposed. We then provided the terms with a translation in English both in the singular and plural form. Subsequently, we conducted a brief exploratory study with DeepL, Google Translate, and Microsoft Bing by back-translating into German the first 20 seed nouns contained in our dataset.

The results from this exploratory study show that all systems default to male forms. Moreover, Google Translate usually provides gender-specific translations in the masculine and feminine, and Microsoft Bing offers synonymous translations in the masculine form only. For these reasons, we further conduct our study with DeepL which usually generates three to four translations per seed word.

In a nutshell, our findings seem to suggest that GFL is starting to appear in DeepL outputs, probably due to the relatively widespread GFL use in German-speaking countries. Nevertheless, DeepL still generates gender-fair forms inconsistently and far more often in the plural. Finally, the gender-inclusive forms found in the machine translations are generally outdated and exclusive of genders beyond the binary – an issue still under-researched within translation studies and computational linguistics with few exceptions (Saunders et al., 2020; Lauscher et al., 2023; Lardelli and Gromann, 2023a).

## Acknowledgements

This work is part of the GeFMT project (13223) sponsored by the European Association for Machine Translation (EAMT) under the EAMT Sponsorship of Activities 2023.

## References

[Atkins1996] Atkins, Beryl T Sue. 1996. Bilingual dictionaries: Past, present and future. *EURALEX'96 Proceedings. Göteborg: Department of Swedish, Göteborg University*, pages 515–546.

[Attanasio et al.2023] Attanasio, Giuseppe, Flor Miriam Plaza del Arco, Debora Nozza, and Anne Lauscher. 2023. A tale of pronouns: Interpretability informs gender bias mitigation for fairer instruction-tuned machine translation. In Bouamor, Houda, Juan Pino, and Kalika Bali, editors, *Proceedings of the 2023 Conference on Empirical Methods in Natural Language Processing*, pages 3996–4014, Singapore, December. Association for Computational Linguistics.

[Barocas et al.2017] Barocas, Solon, Kate Crawford, Aaron Shapiro, and Hanna Wallach. 2017. The problem with bias: Allocative versus representational harms in machine learning. In *9th Annual conference of the special interest group for computing, information and society*. Philadelphia, PA, USA.

[Cao and Daumé III2020] Cao, Yang Trista and Hal Daumé III. 2020. Toward gender-inclusive coreference resolution. In Jurafsky, Dan, Joyce Chai, Natalie Schluter, and Joel Tetreault, editors, *Proceedings of the 58th Annual Meeting of the Association for Computational Linguistics*, pages 4568–4595, Online, July. Association for Computational Linguistics.

[Ciora et al.2021] Ciora, Chloe, Nur Iren, and Malihe Alikhani. 2021. Examining covert gender bias: A case study in Turkish and English machine translation models. In Belz, Anya, Angela Fan, Ehud Reiter, and Yaji Sripada, editors, *Proceedings of the 14th International Conference on Natural Language Generation*, pages 55–63, Aberdeen, Scotland, UK, August. Association for Computational Linguistics.

[Corbett1991] Corbett, Greville G. 1991. *Gender*. Cambridge University Press.

[Cotelli Kureth et al.2023] Cotelli Kureth, Sara, Alice Delorme Benites, Mara Haller, Hasti Noghrechi, and Elizabeth Steele. 2023. "i looked it up in deepl": Machine translation and digital tools in the language classroom. *Studie e Ricerche: Human Translation and Natural Language Processing Towards a New Consensus?*, 35:81–96.

[Daems2023] Daems, Joke. 2023. Gender-inclusive translation for a gender-inclusive sport: strategies and translator perceptions at the international quadball association. In Vanmassenhove, Eva, Beatrice Savoldi, Luisa Bentivogli, Joke Daems, and Janiça Hackenbuchner, editors, *Proceedings of the First Workshop on Gender-Inclusive Translation Technologies*, pages 37–47, Tampere, Finland, June. European Association for Machine Translation.

[Deutscher2010] Deutscher, Guy. 2010. *Through the Language Glass: Why the World Looks Different in Other Languages*. Metropolitan Books.

[Dev et al.2021] Dev, Sunipa, Masoud Monajatipoor, Anaelia Ovalle, Arjun Subramonian, Jeff Phillips, and Kai-Wei Chang. 2021. Harms of gender exclusivity and challenges in non-binary representation in language technologies. In Moens, Marie-Francine, Xuanjing Huang, Lucia Specia, and Scott Wen-tau Yih, editors, *Proceedings of the 2021 Conference on Empirical Methods in Natural Language Processing*, pages 1968–1994, Online and Punta Cana, Dominican Republic, November. Association for Computational Linguistics.

[Duan et al.2020] Duan, Xiangyu, Baijun Ji, Hao Jia, Min Tan, Min Zhang, Boxing Chen, Weihua Luo, and Yue Zhang. 2020. Bilingual dictionary based neural machine translation without using parallel sentences. In Jurafsky, Dan, Joyce Chai, Natalie Schluter, and Joel Tetreault, editors, *Proceedings of the 58th Annual Meeting of the Association for Computational Linguistics*, pages 1570–1579, Online, July. Association for Computational Linguistics.

[Gromann et al.2023] Gromann, Dagmar, Manuel Lardelli, Katta Spiel, Sabrina Burtscher, Lukas Daniel Klausner, Arthur Mettinger, Igor Miladinovic, Sigrid Schefer-Wenzl, Daniela Duh, and Katharina Bühn. 2023. Participatory research as a path to community-informed, gender-fair machine translation. In Vanmassenhove, Eva, Beatrice Savoldi, Luisa Bentivogli, Joke Daems, and Janiça Hackenbuchner, editors, *Proceedings of the First Workshop on Gender-Inclusive Translation Technologies*, pages 49–59, Tampere, Finland, June. European Association for Machine Translation.

[Körner et al.2022] Körner, Anita, Bleen Abraham, Ralf Rummer, and Fritz Strack. 2022. Gender representations elicited by the gender star form. *Journal of Language and Social Psychology*, 41(5):553–571.

[Kramer2016] Kramer, Elise. 2016. Feminist linguistics and linguistic feminisms. In Lewin, Ellen and Leni M. Silverstein, editors, *Mapping Feminist Anthropology in the Twenty-first Century*, pages 65–83. Rutgers University Press.

[Kuczmarski2018] Kuczmarski, James. 2018. Reducing gender bias in google translate.

[Lardelli and Gromann2023a] Lardelli, Manuel and Dagmar Gromann. 2023a. Gender-fair post-editing: A case study beyond the binary. In Nurminen, Mary, Judith Brenner, Maarit Koponen, Sirkku Latomaa, Mikhail Mikhailov, Frederike Schierl, Tharindu Ranasinghe, Eva Vanmassenhove, Sergi Alvarez Vidal, Nora Aranberri, Mara Nunziatini, Carla Parra Escartín, Mikel Forcada, Maja Popovic, Carolina Scarton, and Helena Moniz, editors, *Proceedings of the 24th Annual Conference of the European Association for Machine Translation*, pages 251–260, Tampere, Finland, June. European Association for Machine Translation.

[Lardelli and Gromann2023b] Lardelli, Manuel and Dagmar Gromann. 2023b. Translating non-binary coming-out reports: Gender-fair language strategies and use in news articles. *The Journal of Specialised Translation*, 40:213–240.

[Lardelli2023] Lardelli, Manuel. 2023. Gender-fair translation: a case study beyond the binary. *Perspectives*, pages 1–17.

[Lauscher et al.2023] Lauscher, Anne, Debora Nozza, Ehm Miltersen, Archie Crowley, and Dirk Hovy. 2023. What about "em"? how commercial machine translation fails to handle (neo-)pronouns. In Rogers, Anna, Jordan Boyd-Graber, and Naoaki Okazaki, editors, *Proceedings of the 61st Annual Meeting of the Association for Computational Linguistics (Volume 1: Long Papers)*, pages 377–392, Toronto, Canada, July. Association for Computational Linguistics.

[López2019] López, Ártemis. 2019. Tú, yo, elle y el lenguaje no binario. *La Linterna del Traductor*, 19.

[McConnell-Ginet2013] McConnell-Ginet, Sally. 2013. Gender and its relation to sex: The myth of 'natural'gender. In Corbett, Greville G, editor, *The Expression of Gender*, pages 3–38. De Gruyter Mouton.

[Nagata et al.2001] Nagata, Masaaki, Teruka Saito, and Kenji Suzuki. 2001. Using the web as a bilingual dictionary. In *Proceedings of the ACL 2001 Workshop on Data-Driven Methods in Machine Translation*.

[Paolucci et al.2023] Paolucci, Angela Balducci, Manuel Lardelli, and Dagmar Gromann. 2023. Gender-fair language in translation: A case study. In Vanmassenhove, Eva, Beatrice Savoldi, Luisa Bentivogli, Joke Daems, and Janiça Hackenbuchner, editors, *Proceedings of the First Workshop on Gender-Inclusive Translation Technologies*, pages 13–23, Tampere, Finland, June. European Association for Machine Translation.

[Piergentili et al.2023] Piergentili, Andrea, Beatrice Savoldi, Dennis Fucci, Matteo Negri, and Luisa Bentivogli. 2023. Hi guys or hi folks? benchmarking gender-neutral machine translation with the GeNTE corpus. In Bouamor, Houda, Juan Pino, and Kalika Bali, editors, *Proceedings of the 2023 Conference on Empirical Methods in Natural Language Processing*, pages 14124–14140, Singapore, December. Association for Computational Linguistics.

[Prates et al.2020] Prates, Marcelo OR, Pedro H Avelar, and Luís C Lamb. 2020. Assessing gender bias in machine translation: a case study with google translate. *Neural Computing and Applications*, 32:6363–6381.

[Saunders and Olsen2023] Saunders, Danielle and Katrina Olsen. 2023. Gender, names and other mysteries: Towards the ambiguous for gender-inclusive translation. In Vanmassenhove, Eva, Beatrice Savoldi, Luisa Bentivogli, Joke Daems, and Janiça Hackenbuchner, editors, *Proceedings of the First Workshop on Gender-Inclusive Translation Technologies*, pages 85–93, Tampere, Finland, June. European Association for Machine Translation.

[Saunders et al.2020] Saunders, Danielle, Rosie Sallis, and Bill Byrne. 2020. Neural machine translation doesn't translate gender coreference right unless you make it. In Costa-jussà, Marta R., Christian Hardmeier, Will Radford, and Kellie Webster, editors, *Proceedings of the Second Workshop on Gender Bias in Natural Language Processing*, pages 35–43, Barcelona, Spain (Online), December. Association for Computational Linguistics.

[Savoldi et al.2021] Savoldi, Beatrice, Marco Gaido, Luisa Bentivogli, Matteo Negri, and Marco Turchi. 2021. Gender bias in machine translation. *Transactions of the Association for Computational Linguistics*, 9:845–874.

[Savoldi et al.2023] Savoldi, Beatrice, Marco Gaido, Matteo Negri, and Luisa Bentivogli. 2023. Test suites task: Evaluation of gender fairness in MT with MuST-SHE and INES. In Koehn, Philipp, Barry Haddow, Tom Kocmi, and Christof Monz, editors, *Proceedings of the Eighth Conference on Machine Translation*, pages 252–262, Singapore, December. Association for Computational Linguistics.

[Sczesny et al.2016] Sczesny, Sabine, Magda Formanowicz, and Franziska Moser. 2016. Can gender-fair language reduce gender stereotyping and discrimination? *Frontiers in psychology*, 7.

[Simon1996] Simon, Sherry. 1996. *Gender in Translation: Cultural Identity and the Politics of Transmission*. Routledge.

[Stahlberg and Sczesny2001] Stahlberg, Dagmar and Sabine Sczesny. 2001. Effekte des generischen maskulinums und alternativer sprachformen auf den gedanklichen einbezug von frauen. *Psychologische Rundschau*, 52(3):131–140.

[Stahlberg et al.2007] Stahlberg, Dagmar, Friederike Braun, Lisa Irmen, and Sabine Sczesny. 2007. Representation of the sexes in language. *Social Communication*, pages 163–187.

[Stanovsky et al.2019] Stanovsky, Gabriel, Noah A. Smith, and Luke Zettlemoyer. 2019. Evaluating gender bias in machine translation. In Korhonen, Anna, David Traum, and Lluís Màrquez, editors, *Proceedings of the 57th Annual Meeting of the Association for Computational Linguistics*, pages 1679–1684, Florence, Italy, July. Association for Computational Linguistics.

[Thompson1987] Thompson, Geoff. 1987. Using bilingual dictionaries. *ELT journal*, 41(4):282–286.

[Translator2023] Translator, Microsoft. 2023. Bing's gendered translations tackle bias in translation.

[Zhang et al.2021] Zhang, Tong, Long Zhang, Wei Ye, Bo Li, Jinan Sun, Xiaoyu Zhu, Wen Zhao, and Shikun Zhang. 2021. Point, disambiguate and copy: Incorporating bilingual dictionaries for neural machine translation. In Zong, Chengqing, Fei Xia, Wenjie Li, and Roberto Navigli, editors, *Proceedings of the 59th Annual Meeting of the Association for Computational Linguistics and the 11th International Joint Conference on Natural Language Processing (Volume 1: Long Papers)*, pages 3970–3979, Online, August. Association for Computational Linguistics.

# Gender and bias in Amazon review translations: by humans, MT systems and ChatGPT

**Maja Popović[1], Ekaterina Lapshinova-Koltunski[2]**
[1] ADAPT Centre, School of Computing, Dublin City University, Ireland
maja.popovic@adaptcentre.ie
[2] Language and Information Sciences, University of Hildesheim, Germany
lapshinovakoltun@uni-hildesheim.de

## Abstract

This paper presents an analysis of first-person gender in five different translation variants of Amazon product reviews: those produced by professional translators, by translation students, with different machine translation (MT) systems and with ChatGPT. The analysis revealed that the majority of the reviews were translated into the masculine first-person gender both by humans and by machines. Further inspection revealed that the choice of the gender in a translation is not related to the actual gender of the translator. Finally, the analysis of different products showed that there are certain bias tendencies, because the distribution of genders notably differ for different products.

## 1 Introduction

In this paper, we focus on the distribution of gendered words in human and machine translations of product reviews from English into Croatian and Russian. In contrast to English, both Croatian and Russian have gender marking not only on pronouns, but also on nouns, adjectives, verbs, determiners and numbers. The gender implicit in the English source needs to be specified in the target. This may result in translation errors, mismatches and inconsistencies, as well as gender bias in train and test data.

In reviews, the texts are written in the first person form as illustrated in example (1). While translating from English into Croatian or Russian, the gender of the adjectives and verb past and passive participles should be specified: обожал (masculine) vs. обожала (feminine).

(1) a. *I **loved** using this makeup*
b. я обожал(а) пользоваться этой косметикой.

The decision for either feminine or masculine form is required not only in case of machine translation. Human translators need to specify this form, too. If no information on the text author is available and no specific instructions are given for translators, this may result in inconsistencies and individual decisions by human translators.

Therefore, we decide to look into this variation analysing and comparing translations produced by two different groups of translators (professional and student) as well as with two machine translation systems and ChatGPT large language model in the two language pairs at hand.

Our work is similar to the studies of gender bias in machine translation (MT). However, our primary focus is not on reducing the gender bias, but rather on regularities in human and machine translation data that may follow in the emerging gender bias in the data.

Gender bias (preference or toward one gender over the other) exists in training data, pre-trained models such as word embeddings and also algorithms themselves (Zhao et al., 2018a; Bolukbasi et al., 2016; Caliskan et al., 2017; Garg et al.2018), so that a machine translation system containing bias can produce gender biased predictions. Although this issue belong to active research topics, detection and evaluation of gender bias in machine translation systems have not been thoroughly investigated yet.





*Proceedings of the 2nd International Workshop on Gender-Inclusive Translation Technologies*, pages 22–30
June 27, 2024 ©2024 European Association for Machine Translation

In our analysis, we focus on the following research questions:

**RQ1:** What is the distribution of first person gender in different translations?

**RQ2:** Is choice of the gender in human translations related to the gender of the translator?

**RQ3:** Is choice of the gender related to the topic/product?

The remainder of the paper is organised as follows: Section 2 provides and overview of related studies. The data is described in Section 3. The analyses and the results are presented in Sections 4 and 5, and conclusions in Section 6.

## 2 Related Work

Our work is similar to the studies of gender bias in natural language processing and specifically in machine translation. However, our descriptive aims differ from those existing in most studies. Some studies do describe bias in the data. For instance, Zhao et al. (2018) addressed gender bias in word embeddings and Sun et al. (2019) provides an overview of existing biases.

Some works focus on the creation of challenge or test suites. Stanovsky et al. (2019) presented a challenge set and evaluation protocol for the analysis of gender bias in MT. Their automatic gender bias evaluation method was developed for eight target languages (including Russian) with grammatical gender. They tested six MT systems themselves, including also Google. Vanmassenhove and Monti (2021) presented an English–Italian challenge set focusing on the resolution of natural gender phenomena by providing word-level gender tags on the English source side and multiple gender alternative translations, where needed, on the Italian target side. The data analysed in our study can potentially serve as a test suite as well.

In our work, we also address bias dependence on topic or product. Similarly, bias variation was addressed in (Zhao et al., 2017) who found that on the one hand, data sets for specific tasks (e.g. cooking) contain significant gender bias and, on the other hand, models trained on these datasets further amplify existing bias.

Some works showed that bias can be measured, see e.g. (Cho et al., 2019) who proposed a measure called 'translation gender bias index' (TGBI).

We analyse both human and machine-translated texts. The latter were analysed in several other works. For instance, Saunders et al. (2020) explored the potential of gender-inflection controlled translation in case the gender is identifiable either from a human reference or when it can be automatically gender-tagged. The authors found out that simple existing approaches could overgeneralize a gender-feature to multiple entities in a sentence, and suggested effective alternatives in the form of tagged co-reference adaptation data. They also proposed an extension to assess translations of gender-neutral entities from English given a corresponding linguistic convention in the target language. In another study, the authors analyse and evaluate gender bias comparing bias measurements across multiple metrics for pre-trained embeddings and the ones learned by their own machine translation model (Ramesh et al., 2021). A summary of various analyses of gender bias in machine translation was presented by Savoldi et al. (2021). The authors also discussed the mitigating strategies proposed in various studies. Měchura (2022) presented a taxonomy of phenomena which caused bias in machine translation. Interestingly, it included not only gender bias on people being male and female, but also number and formality bias (singular *you* vs. plural *you* as well as informal *you* vs. formal *you*).

In our study, we focus not only on the machine translations but also on the human ones and compare them across each other. We also distinguish two groups of translators according to their experience: professionals and students. In this way, we also consider the bias introduced by the human translators, which has not been thoroughly analysed so far. Human bias has been addressed in a few studies only. For instance, Hada et al. (2023) investigated the generation and consequent receptivity of manual annotators to bias of varying degrees. The authors created the first dataset of GPT-generated English text with normative ratings of gender bias. The variation of themes of gender biases in the observed ranking was then systematically analysed. The authors showed that identity-attack was most closely related to gender bias. They also showed the performance of existing automated models trained on related concepts on their dataset.

We believe that our work has an added value to the studies existing in the area of machine translation and natural language processing, as it adds to the awareness (Daems and Hackenbuchner, 2022) of the bias existing in the translation data, both in human and machine translations.

## 3 Data

For our analysis, we use the publicly available corpus DiHuTra[1] (Lapshinova-Koltunski et al., 2022). The corpus contains 196 English Amazon product reviews (14 reviews in each of 14 different product categories) and their human and machine translations into three languages, Croatian, Russian and Finnish. Since the Finnish language does not have grammatical gender in any word category, not even in personal pronouns, only Croatian and Russian were included in our analysis. The number of running words and vocabulary size for the source text and for each of the translations can be seen in Table 1.

In most of the reviews, the gender of the writer is not known, and not specified by any information in the English source. In two reviews only, the text indicates that the writer was a female. The human translations were produced by two groups of translators: several professional translators and several students. The translators were only instructed to keep the given segmentation and not to use any MT system. They did not receive any guidelines about how to treat the gender in the target language. Therefore, the corpus is appropriate to explore the subjectivity.

The machine translations in the corpus were generated by different MT systems. Croatian MT outputs are the two best ranked outputs by human evaluation from the WMT 2022 shared task[2] (Kocmi et al., 2022). Russian MT outputs were generated using Google Translate[3] and DeepL Translator[4]. ChatGPT [5] translations for all target languages were generated using the publicly available GPT 3.5 version. Since human translators were given only simple instructions, a similar approach was used for ChatGPT as well, namely a simple prompt "translate into Croatian/Russian".

[1]http://hdl.handle.net/21.11119/0000-000A-1BA9-A

[2]https://www.statmt.org/wmt22/translation-task.html

[3]https://translate.google.com/, accessed in February 2023

[4]https://www.deepl.com/en/translator, accessed in August 2023

[5]https://chat.openai.com/, accessed in November 2023

| text | running words | vocabulary |
|---|---|---|
| en source | 15,236 | 3,155 |
| hr prof | 13,981 | 4,359 |
| hr stud | 13,931 | 4,446 |
| hr mt1 | 13,467 | 4,309 |
| hr mt2 | 13,465 | 4,247 |
| hr gpt3.5 | 14,170 | 4,265 |
| ru prof | 14,217 | 4,414 |
| ru stud | 14,247 | 4,523 |
| ru mt1 | 14,472 | 4,348 |
| ru mt2 | 14,635 | 4,391 |
| ru gpt3.5 | 15,015 | 4,397 |

**Table 1:** Corpus statistics.

## 4 Analysis of first-person gender

As mentioned in Section 3, the gender of the writer is not known, and with the exception of two reviews, not specified by any information in the English source. Therefore, the choice of the first person gender in the translation is totally free. The analysis of first-person gender was carried out manually, finding that the majority of the first-person gendered words are verb past participles, followed by adjectives and verb passive participles. This analysis revealed that some student translations and many ChatGPT translations contain the inclusive gender forms. These words were not properly recognised by the part-of-speech tagger and were tagged as masculine nouns.

For each review, a gender label was assigned according to the gendered words it contained. If all first-person gendered words within a review have the same gender (feminine, masculine or inclusive), the review was assigned this gender label. If there was a mixture of first-person genders, the review got the label "mixed".

An example of gender labels for Croatian and Russian translations[6] is shown in Table 2. The English source text contains two words referring to the first person (one verb past participle *received* and one adjective *upset*) which should be gendered in the translations. The first translation is labelled as feminine since both relevant words are in the feminine form. Analogously, the second translation is labelled as masculine, and the third one as inclusive. The fourth and fifth translation are labelled as mixed, because the two relevant words have different genders.

[6]Sentences are shown instead of entire reviews for the sake of space and clarity.

| | | |
|---|---|---|
| | en | this is fake MAC, i just **received** mine and super **upset** to find out it isnt real MAc. |
| *fem.* | hr | Ovo je fejk MAC, upravo sam **dobila** svoj i jako sam **ljuta** što nije pravi MAC. |
| | ru | Это подделка MAC, я только что получила свою косметику и ужасно расстроена, потому что это не настоящая косметика MAC! |
| *masc.* | hr | Ovo je fejk MAC, upravo sam **dobio** svoj i jako sam **ljut** što nije pravi MAC. |
| | ru | Это подделка MAC, я только что получил свою косметику и ужасно расстроен, потому что это не настоящая косметика MAC! |
| *incl.* | hr | Ovo je fejk MAC, upravo sam **dobio/la** svoj i jako sam **ljut/a** što nije pravi MAC. |
| | ru | Это подделка MAC, я только что получил(а) свою косметику и ужасно расстроен(а), потому что это не настоящая косметика MAC! |
| *mixed* | hr | Ovo je fejk MAC, upravo sam **dobila** svoj i jako sam **ljut** što nije pravi MAC. |
| | ru | Это подделка MAC, я только что получил свою косметику и ужасно расстроена, потому что это не настоящая косметика MAC! |
| *mixed* | hr | Ovo je fejk MAC, upravo sam **dobio/la** svoj i jako sam **ljut** što nije pravi MAC. |
| | ru | Это подделка MAC, я только что получила свою косметику и ужасно расстроен(а), потому что это не настоящая косметика MAC! |

**Table 2:** Example of gender labels according to first-person gendered words.

It should be noted that there are still no non-binary forms in the analysed target languages. Neuter gender is never used for people, only for objects, and would sound awkward, and even possibly offensive. Also, while in some texts it is possible to avoid the gender and generate a "neutral" translation, it is very difficult to avoid all adjectives and past participles. The only way for a proper inclusion is to use the "inclusive" form, comprising both gender variants in a word.

## 5 Results

### 5.1 Distribution of first-person gender

First of all, it was found out that about two thirds of the translated reviews (slightly more in Croatian than in Russian) are found to contain indicators of the writer's gender. The rest does not contain any indicator of the writer's gender and was not taken into account in the analysis.

The gender distribution of the gendered reviews is shown in Figure 1: feminine reviews are presented in red, masculine in blue, inclusive in orange, and mixed in grey. For each gender category, lighter nuance represents Croatian and darker nuance Russian.

It can be seen that masculine first-person gender is dominant for both languages and all translation variants, both human and machine-generated. The difference between the percentage of masculine and feminine reviews is smaller in human translations, but still notable. For both target languages, there are slightly less feminine reviews in student translations than in professional ones.

As for machine-generated translations, distributions are slightly different for different systems and target languages, but the overall tendency is the same: the vast majority of the reviews are written in masculine. The most extreme are Russian ChatGPT translations with only 0.5% of all gendered reviews being written in the feminine gender.

The inclusive reviews are mainly found in Croatian ChatGPT translations, although there are a few Russian ones, too. One Croatian student also opted to use the inclusive form. The rest of translations (MT outputs, professional translations, Russian student translations) do not contain any inclusive reviews.

Mixed reviews were found in all machine-generated translations, more in Croatian than in Russian. The smallest amount of mixed reviews was found in the Russian ChatGPT output (0.5%, the same as feminine reviews). It should be noted that in ChatGPT translations there was no mixing of masculine and feminine forms as in MT outputs, but of inclusive and masculine or feminine forms.

Overall, even human translations "prefer" to write in masculine gender, and the "preference" is even stronger in MT systems and ChatGPT, especially Russian ChatGPT.

As for the two reviews with indicators of a female author, all human translators used the feminine gender, while most MT translations had mixed gender. As for ChatGPT, both Russian translations were feminine, while one Croatian

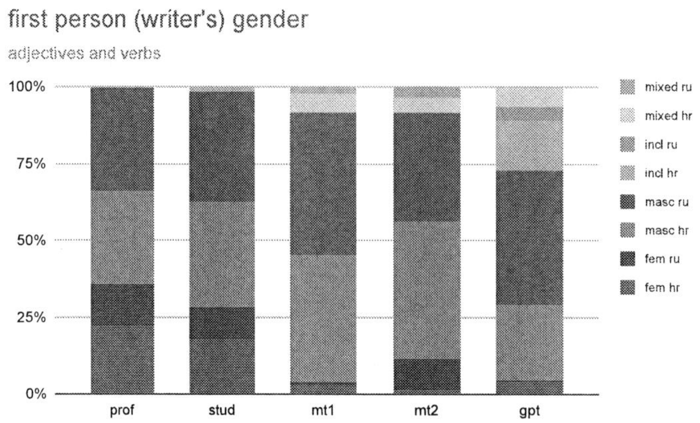


**Figure 1:** Distribution of first-person genders in different translations: red = feminine, blue = masculine, orange = inclusive, grey = mixed; darker shade = Russian, lighter shade = Croatian.

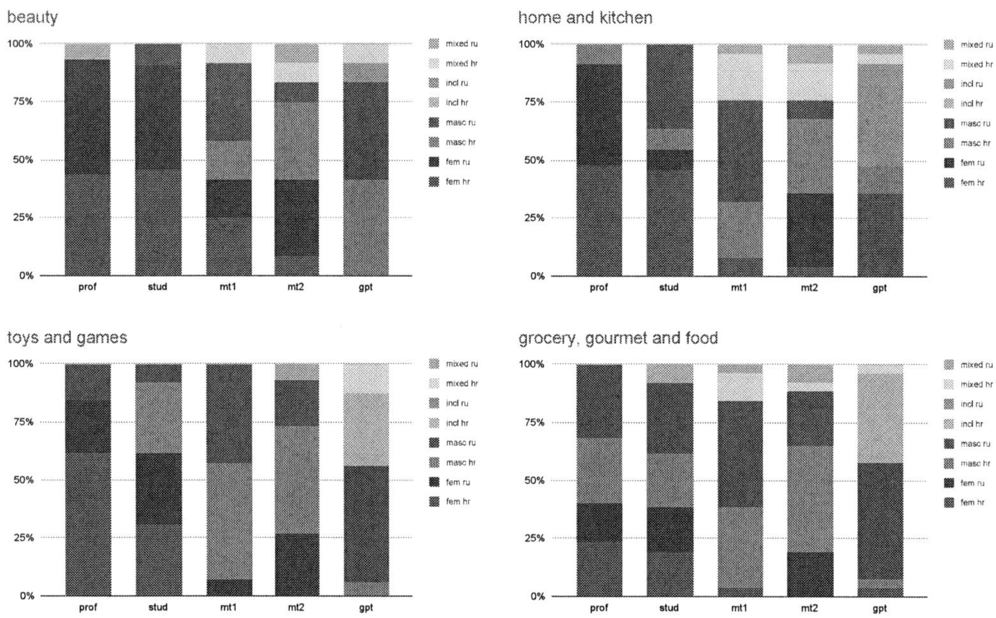


**Figure 2:** Distribution of first person gender for different products, part 1.

translation was masculine and one mixed, containing feminine and inclusive forms.

## 5.2 Translators' gender

In order to analyse the preference for masculine gender in human translations, we looked into the meta-data which provide the actual gender of the translator for each review. Overall, there were more female than male translators, and consequently more reviews translated by female translators, which already indicated that the translators do not necessarily use their own gender in translations.

Table 3 presents the percentage of translated reviews written in particular gender for each group of the translators. For example, the first row should be interpreted in the following way: of all Croatian professional translations, 50 reviews were translated by a male translator. Of these reviews, 44% were written in masculine gender (meaning that the translator kept his own gender) and 34% in feminine gender (meaning that the translator changed his own gender).

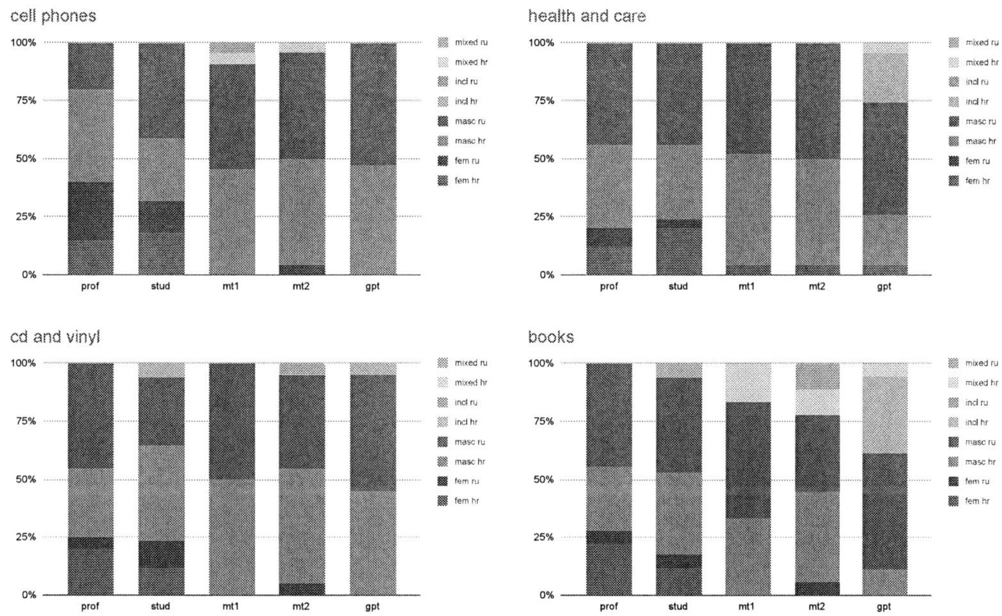


**Figure 3:** Distribution of first person gender for different products, part 2.

| translator | | | | translations | | |
|---|---|---|---|---|---|---|
| | | | number of | gender | | |
| group | lang. | gender | reviews | masc. | fem. | incl. |
| prof. | hr | m | 50 | 44.0 | 34.0 | 0 |
| | | f | 146 | 39.7 | 28.8 | 0 |
| | ru | m | 20 | 40.0 | 20.0 | 0 |
| | | f | 176 | 45.4 | 18.2 | 0 |
| stud. | hr | m | 51 | 54.9 | 17.6 | 0 |
| | | f | 145 | 40.7 | 25.5 | 2.8 |
| | ru | m | 0 | 0 | 0 | 0 |
| | | f | 196 | 46.4 | 39.8 | 0 |

**Table 3:** Translators' reported gender and percentage of gender chosen for the translations.

In total, the numbers in Table 3 shows that translators choose masculine gender more often, regardless of their actual gender.

### 5.3 Tendencies for different products

Since the previous analysis showed that both female and male translators "prefer" the masculine writer's gender, we decided to look into the gender distributions for different products.

We have to point out that there are only 14 reviews for each of the 14 products, and not all of them are gendered, so that it is not possible to draw any hard conclusions from this analysis, but certain tendencies can definitively be observed. Figures 2, 3 and 4 show the distributions for each of the products, ordered by the proportion of feminine reviews in human translations.

The main observation is that there are clear differences in gender distributions for certain products (namely bias), and that the product-related differences are even more notable in human translations.

Regarding **human translations**, almost all "beauty" reviews are feminine, followed by "home and kitchen" and "toys and games" (Figure 2, while there are only a few feminine translations of "sports and outdoors", "movies and TV" as well as "patio, lawn and garden", and there is no single feminine review for "musical instruments" (Figure 4).

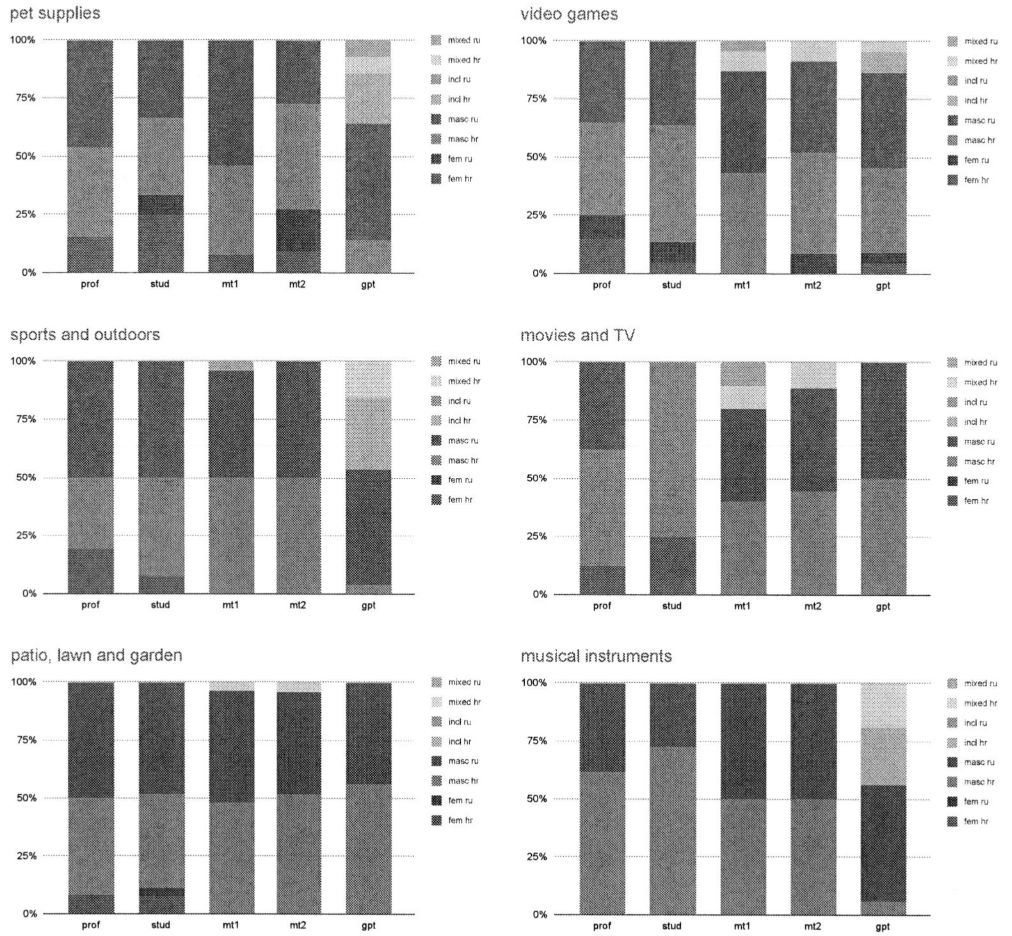


**Figure 4:** Distribution of first person gender for different products, part 3.

As for **machine-generated translations**, there are less feminine reviews than in human translations for each of the products. For example, for the category "beauty", gender in machine translations is balanced, while the predominant gender in human translations is feminine. For the 'middle-range' products such as "cell phones" or "books", there are about 25-35% of feminine reviews in human translations, but very few or none in machine-generated ones. Finally, for "patio, lawn and garden" there are some feminine reviews in human translations but none in machine-generated ones, and for "musical instruments" there is no single feminine review at all. It should be noted, however, that there are inclusive Croatian ChatGPT outputs.

Another interesting observation is that Russian ChatGPT inclusive reviews are only found in the predominantly "feminine" products, namely "beauty" and "home and kitchen", while there no clear product-related tendencies could be observed for the Croatian ChatGPT inclusive translations.

## 6 Conclusions

This work presents results of analysis of first-person gender in Russian and Croatian translations of English user reviews. We addressed three research questions concerning the distribution of the first person gender, the relation between the choice of the gender for translation and the real gender of the translator, as well as a tendency towards a product or product group bias. We group the findings according to the three research questions addressed:

**RQ1:** What is the distribution of first person gender in different translations?

We could observe that in all translations, the predominant gender is masculine. Interestingly, the difference is much stronger in machine-translated texts. This indicates the intensification of the gender bias existing in human translations.

**RQ2:** Is choice of the gender in human translations related to the gender of the translator?

Our data shows that it is not the case. All translators in our dataset at hand, regardless of their gender, translated more reviews into the masculine form. It is interesting to note that we also observed the cases of a male translator using feminine forms.

**RQ3:** Is choice of the gender related to the topic/product?

Although the data set is too small to draw hard conclusions, we noticed a clear tendency, especially in human translations. Similar tendencies are observed in machine-generated output, although the overall trend is notably less feminine translations in each of the product categories.

The reported findings also open several directions for future work. Apart from including more target languages from different families, as well as more domains and topics, more language models should be included, also the outputs using different prompts such as giving particular instructions regarding gender specification.

Furthermore, a test suite specifically designed for first-gender analysis should be used in future experiments.

## Limitations

First of all, our analysis includes only two target languages belonging to the same language family. Furthermore, only one domain was analysed on a relatively small corpus. Therefore, the analysis of different products/topics, although showing some clear tendencies, is not fully reliable. Furthermore, the corpus is not designed for gender evaluation, so that only two thirds of the corpus were actually convenient for the experiment. Due to the nature of the two languages, only two genders were included. However, the possibilities for inclusive language were discussed.

As for ChatGPT translations, we used the version based on GPT-3.5 instead of the newest one based on GPT-4. However, the free version is still based on GPT-3.5, so that a large number of users are still using this one.

## Acknowledgements

ADAPT, the SFI Research Centre for AI-Driven Digital Content Technology, is funded by Science Foundation Ireland through the SFI Research Centres Programme under Grant Agreement No. 13/RC/2106_P2.

## References

Cho, Won Ik, Ji Won Kim, Seok Min Kim, and Nam Soo Kim. 2019. On measuring gender bias in translation of gender-neutral pronouns. In *Proceedings of the First Workshop on Gender Bias in Natural Language Processing*, pages 173–181, Florence, Italy, August. Association for Computational Linguistics.

Daems, Joke and Janiça Hackenbuchner. 2022. DeBiasByUs: Raising awareness and creating a database of MT bias. In Moniz, Helena, Lieve Macken, Andrew Rufener, Loïc Barrault, Marta R. Costa-jussà, Christophe Declercq, Maarit Koponen, Ellie Kemp, Spyridon Pilos, Mikel L. Forcada, Carolina Scarton, Joachim Van den Bogaert, Joke Daems, Arda Tezcan, Bram Vanroy, and Margot Fonteyne, editors, *Proceedings of the 23rd Annual Conference of the European Association for Machine Translation*, pages 289–290, Ghent, Belgium, June. European Association for Machine Translation.

Hada, Rishav, Agrima Seth, Harshita Diddee, and Kalika Bali. 2023. "Fifty shades of bias": Normative ratings of gender bias in GPT generated English text. In Bouamor, Houda, Juan Pino, and Kalika Bali, editors, *Proceedings of the 2023 Conference on Empirical Methods in Natural Language Processing*, pages 1862–1876, Singapore, December. Association for Computational Linguistics.

Kocmi, Tom, Rachel Bawden, Ondřej Bojar, Anton Dvorkovich, Christian Federmann, Mark Fishel, Thamme Gowda, Yvette Graham, Roman Grundkiewicz, Barry Haddow, Rebecca Knowles, Philipp Koehn, Christof Monz, Makoto Morishita, Masaaki Nagata, Toshiaki Nakazawa, Michal Novák, Martin Popel, and Maja Popović. 2022. Findings of the 2022 conference on machine translation (WMT22). In *Proceedings of WMT-2022*, Abu Dhabi, United Arab Emirates (Hybrid), December.

Lapshinova-Koltunski, Ekaterina, Maja Popović, and Maarit Koponen. 2022. DiHuTra: a Parallel Corpus to Analyse Differences between Human Translations. In *Proceedings of LREC-2022*, pages 1751–1760, Marseille, France, 20-25 June. ELDA.

Měchura, Michal. 2022. A taxonomy of bias-causing ambiguities in machine translation. In *Proceedings of the 4th Workshop on Gender Bias in Natural Language Processing (GeBNLP)*, pages 168–173, Seattle, Washington, July. Association for Computational Linguistics.

Ramesh, Krithika, Gauri Gupta, and Sanjay Singh. 2021. Evaluating gender bias in Hindi-English machine translation. In *Proceedings of the 3rd Workshop on Gender Bias in Natural Language Processing*, pages 16–23, Online, August. Association for Computational Linguistics.

Saunders, Danielle, Rosie Sallis, and Bill Byrne. 2020. Neural machine translation doesn't translate gender coreference right unless you make it. In *Proceedings of the Second Workshop on Gender Bias in Natural Language Processing*, pages 35–43, Barcelona, Spain (Online), December. Association for Computational Linguistics.

Savoldi, Beatrice, Marco Gaido, Luisa Bentivogli, Matteo Negri, and Marco Turchi. 2021. Gender bias in machine translation. *Transactions of the Association for Computational Linguistics*, 9:845–874.

Stanovsky, Gabriel, Noah A. Smith, and Luke Zettlemoyer. 2019. Evaluating gender bias in machine translation. In *Proceedings of the 57th Annual Meeting of the Association for Computational Linguistics*, pages 1679–1684, Florence, Italy, July. Association for Computational Linguistics.

Sun, Tony, Andrew Gaut, Shirlyn Tang, Yuxin Huang, Mai ElSherief, Jieyu Zhao, Diba Mirza, Elizabeth Belding, Kai-Wei Chang, and William Yang Wang. 2019. Mitigating gender bias in natural language processing: Literature review. In *Proceedings of the 57th Annual Meeting of the Association for Computational Linguistics*, pages 1630–1640, Florence, Italy, July. Association for Computational Linguistics.

Vanmassenhove, Eva and Johanna Monti. 2021. gENder-IT: An annotated English-Italian parallel challenge set for cross-linguistic natural gender phenomena. In *Proceedings of the 3rd Workshop on Gender Bias in Natural Language Processing*, pages 1–7, Online, August. Association for Computational Linguistics.

Zhao, Jieyu, Tianlu Wang, Mark Yatskar, Vicente Ordonez, and Kai-Wei Chang. 2017. Men also like shopping: Reducing gender bias amplification using corpus-level constraints. In *Proceedings of the 2017 Conference on Empirical Methods in Natural Language Processing*, pages 2979–2989, Copenhagen, Denmark, September. Association for Computational Linguistics.

Zhao, Jieyu, Yichao Zhou, Zeyu Li, Wei Wang, and Kai-Wei Chang. 2018. Learning gender-neutral word embeddings. In *Proceedings of the 2018 Conference on Empirical Methods in Natural Language Processing*, pages 4847–4853, Brussels, Belgium, October-November. Association for Computational Linguistics.

# You Shall Know a Word's Gender by the Company it Keeps: Comparing the Role of Context in Human Gender Assumptions with MT

**Janiça Hackenbuchner, Arda Tezcan, Aaron Maladry** and **Joke Daems**
Language and Translation Technology Team
Ghent University
Groot-Brittanniëlaan 45, 9000 Ghent, Belgium
firstname.lastname@ugent.be

## Abstract

In this paper, we analyse to what extent machine translation (MT) systems and humans base their gender translations and associations on role names and on stereotypicality in the absence of (generic) grammatical gender cues in language. We compare an MT system's choice of gender for a certain word when translating from a notional gender language, English, into a grammatical gender language, German, with the gender associations of humans. We outline a comparative case study of gender translation and annotation of words in isolation, out-of-context, and words in sentence contexts. The analysis reveals patterns of gender (bias) by MT and gender associations by humans for certain (1) out-of-context words and (2) words in-context. Our findings reveal the impact of context on gender choice and translation and show that word-level analyses fall short in such studies.

## 1 Introduction

Aligned with a growing interest and use of language technologies as well as a demand for gender inclusiveness in society, gender bias in Machine Translation (MT) systems and Large Language Models (LLMs) is an increasingly studied phenomenon with varying research approaches. Due to the nature of how MT systems, and Natural Language Processing (NLP) systems in general, are trained based on large language corpora, these systems exhibit and exacerbate biases present in these corpora (Vanmassenhove, 2024). With biases being an inherently useful characteristic for machine learning systems to generalise on unseen data (Mitchell, 1980), they can lead to unfair and harmful stereotypes, such as when referring to a person using an inaccurate gender (Vanmassenhove, 2024).

Previous research on potential triggers of gender bias in MT is often limited to word-level analyses and does not take context into account. The study presented in this paper is part of a broader research project that aims to fill gaps in current studies by focusing on the influence of sentence context on gender translations (Hackenbuchner et al., forthcoming). MT systems primarily translate into generic masculine (Monti, 2020), however, we hypothesise that context can be a deciding factor for MT systems, as well as for humans, to change the gender inflection in their output. To raise awareness of why this might be happening or of where MT should be adapting gender, the goal of a broader research project, of which this study is a part of, is the creation of a detection system that analyses English source data to detect and mark words and phrases that are considered to influence the gender inflection in target translations. In comparison to what MT systems do, it is important to understand how humans perceive gender of words in isolation, out-of-context, and how those perceptions change for words in context. Humans would be well aided to have additional support when machine translating text to ascertain correct and fair gender translations.

The study presented in this paper compares gender bias in MT systems with inherent gender associations perceived by humans. We comparatively analysed (1) how an MT system translates a person's gender of a word out-of-context (i.e. in iso-





*Proceedings of the 2nd International Workshop on Gender-Inclusive Translation Technologies*, pages 31–41
June 27, 2024 ©2024 European Association for Machine Translation

lation) versus in a sentence context, (2) the individual differences between human annotators of gender associations of words out-of-context and in-context, and (3) the comparison of MT with human associations with a focus on gender.

In the following sections, we cover related research (Section 2), how the data was collected (Section 3), the process of participatory data annotation (Section 4), data analysis of both human annotators and MT outputs (Section 5), limitations (Section 7) and a conclusion (Section 6).

## 2 Related Research

Research shows that humans are strongly influenced by how gender is expressed in languages, by role names and by general stereotypes (Gygax et al., 2008; Lardelli and Gromann, 2023; Misersky et al., 2014). Humans construct their own individual representations of gender, which, if available, they base on grammar in language (e.g., *waitress*) but when lacking grammatical cues, they base on stereotype information (Gygax et al., 2008). In grammatical gender languages, such as German (Stahlberg et al., 2007), people are often referred to in the generic masculine which is intended to be *generic* but is not typically interpreted as such (Gygax et al., 2008). Stereotypicality and bias further come into play when language has no grammatical gender cues, lacks pronouns or other gender referents, and the gender interpretation is up to the reader to define or an MT system to translate. Based on previous research, we analysed to what extent, in the absence of grammatical gender cues, MT systems and humans base their gender translations and associations on role names and on stereotypicality.

Previous studies on gender in monolingual English data focused on gender inherently manifested in word embeddings by measuring the gender-inflection on a word level (Bolukbasi et al., 2016; Caliskan et al., 2022). This has not yet been applied to sentence level nor in the context of MT. Previous research on gender in MT includes the creation of challenge sets to test gender bias in MT outputs, for instance based on professions and adjectives, to balance out the gender of these pre-determined words in machine translations (Stanovsky et al., 2019; Saunders and Byrne, 2020; Troles and Schmid, 2021). Such challenge sets follow the format of, for example, containing a female and a male sentence for *"The choreographer finished her work. / The choreographer finished his work."* to fine-tune and therefore balance an MT system on both gendered versions (Saunders and Byrne, 2020). Moreover, existing work on gender bias in MT has predominantly focused on translations of the binary gender, namely male and female, not taking into account the non-binary community, with the exception of few approaches taken, as by Savoldi et al. (2024), Lardelli and Gromann (2023) and Saunders et al. (2021).

A recent study on the comparison of human and model evaluations of gender bias concluded that, under constrained settings, "model biases reflect human decision-making" and that humans make (sometimes wrong) predictions based on societal and cognitive presupposition (Lior and Stanovsky, 2023). In the study presented here, we analyse to what extent MT gender translations (model choices) coincide with human associations of gender.

Starting with words taken out-of-context whose word embeddings have an inherent gender-inflection as well as a list of sentences featuring these words in varying contexts, this research focuses on how differently or similarly humans and MT associate gender with certain words on an individual out-of-context level and how this gender-inflection is affected by sentence context. In this way, we expand on previous research but broaden the scope by collecting natural contexts that influence gender-inflections in translations rather than artificially constructed test sentences, and by extending the gender categories to include non-binary.

## 3 Data Description

The data used for this study is in English, a notional gender language (McConnell-Ginet, 2013), where role names generally do not have a gender assigned, e.g., *poet*, apart from kinship relations (*mother, father*) or a few exceptions (*actor, actress*). English data was filtered from monolingual English corpora (StatMT's news-crawl[1], as well as c4 (Raffel et al., 2019) and wiki (Foundation, nd) as made available on HuggingFace[2]). The MT output is analysed in German, a grammatical gender language (McConnell-Ginet, 2013), where gender is specified.

[1] https://data.statmt.org/news-crawl/
[2] https://huggingface.co/

Compiled List of Individual Words

| | | | | | | |
|---|---|---|---|---|---|---|
| coordinator | **flight attendant** | *musician* | *opponent* | **socialite** | **therapist**° | **lover**° |
| *mechanic* | **dancer**° | visitor | colleague | companion | **author**° | **clerk**° |
| **student** | **accountant** | **designer**° | **baker** | **writer**° | **consumer** | **poet** |
| **bookkeeper** | **counselor** | friend | *guard* | *officer*° | *user* | *supporter* |
| *judge* | *fighter* | *dealer* | *soldier* | *player* | *manager* | *contractor* |
| *captain* | *farmer* | *maestro* | *boss* | *driver* | *idiot* | *cook* |
| *filmmaker* | *admirer* | *follower* | *salesperson* | *buddy* | **winner**° | *construction worker* |

**Table 1:** Individual list of 49 words where those words with a female word embedding gender-inflection are marked in bold, those words with a male gender-inflection are marked in italics, and all others have a neutral gender-inflection. All words with a superscript° appeared more than once in the sentence-context.

### 3.1 Compiling Gender-Ambiguous Words and Sentences

Our focus lay on compiling a list of words, role names, referring to people where the gender is not specified in English (e.g., *poet*) but, as previous research outlined above has shown, their word embeddings are indeed often gender-inflected, which influences MT systems' choice of gender when translating from a notional gender language to a grammatical gender language.

To further analyse the impact of context, this study is based on the annotation and translation of selected words both on an individual level and in varying sentence contexts, in which gender is ambiguous. In total, 150 words were compiled, where 50 had a female-inflected word embedding, 50 were male-inflected and 50 were considered neutral (having neither a measurable female nor male gender inflection). The initial word list was compiled based on previous studies, outlined above and on gender-inflections in word embeddings. In addition, this list was further augmented by prompting ChatGPT for lists of female-inflected, male-inflected and neutral-inflected words. The ChatGPT prompted lists were compared with previous research and where words did not overlap, they were added.

These words were then translated from English into German using the DeepL API between February and March 2024. The German MT output was noted and the gender inflection of the MT was documented, i.e. whether *poet* was translated as *Dichter* (male) or *Dichterin* (female).

These 150 words were used to automatically filter the monolingual English corpora (newscrawl, c4 and wiki) for sentences containing these words. This resulting data was then manually filtered for gender-ambiguous sentences excluding those sentences that contain a gender cue, a pronoun or name referring to the person in question. In total, 892 gender-ambiguous sentences have been collected.

Similarly, all these gender-ambiguous sentences were translated from English into German using the DeepL API between February and March 2024. The gender of the word in the output sentence was noted, i.e. whether the sentence *Who's the worst poet in Miami?* was translated as *Wer ist der schlechteste Dichter in Miami?* (male) or as *Wer ist die schlechteste Dichterin in Miami?* (female). Of these 892 gender-ambiguous sentences, 75% were translated by DeepL into (the generic) male, only 6.6% were translated into female and the rest were mistranslated or translated as neutral (e.g., *the pilot* as *das Pilotprojekt*).

From all sentences, a sample of 60 sentences was selected for this study. These 60 sentences were selected based on the fact that their German machine translation gender-inflections showed a broader distribution, i.e. some sentences were translated as male, some as female. As a result, 18% of the sentences were translated as female and 82% as generic masculine. The focus lay on the gender-ambiguous role names (e.g., *poet*) in the sentences. There were 49 different role names, of which 19 words had a female word embedding gender-inflection, 25 a male gender-inflection and 4 a neutral gender-inflection. This is depicted in Table 1.

There were only 49 individual role names in the 60 sentences because some occurred in different sentences. The difference in gender perceptions for the same word (role name) in different sentence contexts is an interesting factor, further outlined in section 5 and will be further analysed in

Gender-Inflections by MT

| | | | | | | |
|---|---|---|---|---|---|---|
| **coordinator** | *flight attendant* | **musician** | **opponent** | ***socialite*** | **therapist**[1] | **lover**[1] |
| **mechanic** | dancer[1] | **visitor** | colleague | ***companion*** | author[1] | clerk[1] |
| student | accountant | designer[1] | baker | writer[1] | consumer | poet |
| bookkeeper | counselor | **friend** | **guard** | officer[1] | user | supporter |
| judge | fighter | dealer | soldier | player | manager | contractor |
| captain | farmer | maestro | boss | driver | idiot | cook |
| filmmaker | admirer | follower | salesperson | buddy | winner[1] | construction worker |
| officer[2] | therapist[2] | lover[2] | author[2] | writer[2] | designer[2] | clerk[2] |
| dancer[2] | winner[2] | winner[3] | author[3] | | | |

**Table 2:** Gender-inflections by the MT system of words in and out-of-context. All words in italic were female-inflected out-of-context. All words in bold were female-inflected in-context. All other words were male. Superscript 1, 2 and 3 are used to refer to in-context sentence 1, 2 or 3 when there are multiple sentences for a word.

the broader research project, of which this study is a part of (Hackenbuchner et al., forthcoming). An example would be the analysis of the gender association and translation of the word *therapist* in the following two contexts:

- Kensington massage **therapist** jailed for sexually assaulting clients.
- There are 52 weeks in a year, my **therapist** continued matter-of-factly, "I know you can't go on a date every single week, but how many do you think you should be going on?"

We wanted to analyse whether, for the same word, the two different contexts affected the choice of gender. For this example, as depicted in Appendix B, the MT system translated the therapist as female in the first sentence and as male in the second sentence. We want to analyse such differences and whether the choice of gender by human annotators coincides with the gender selected by MT (which in this case it does not as humans annotated the therapist as male in the first context and as female in the second).

### 3.2 Translation Comparison of Words and Sentences

After the data was compiled, a comparison was drawn between the translation of the individual word out-of-context with the translation of the word in a sentence context. This comparison is depicted in Table 2. We can clearly see that the words were predominantly translated as (generic) masculine both in- and out-of-context. Out-of-context, the MT predominantly translated words as male and a mere three words (*flight attendant, socialite, companion*) were translated as female. In sentence context, the MT translated fewer words as male, with a slightly lesser majority of 82%, and in 18% of the cases, as female. We can therefore see that out-of-context, the MT predominantly translates into the male gender inflection. In a sentence context, the MT still predominantly translates into the male gender inflection but to a lesser extent. This shows that the MT, for certain sentences and role names, is influenced by context. Words that the MT had individually translated as male but in a sentence context as female are: *coordinator, mechanic, musician, visitor, friend, opponent, guard, therapist, lover*. The sentences are depicted in Appendix B.

| | out-of-context | in-context |
|---|---|---|
| male | .95 | .82 |
| female | .05 | .18 |

**Table 3:** Label distribution gender-associations of MT translations in-context and out-of-context.

The MT's translation behaviour of gender is later compared to human gender associations of the same words both out-of-context and in a sentence context.

## 4 Annotation & Guidelines

### 4.1 Annotators

Unlike regular annotation tasks where correct word categories are requested to be annotated, the annotations for this research are highly subjective and individual as there was, e.g., no pre-defined part of speech (POS) that had to be annotated. There were no *right* or *wrong* annotations. To cover a variety of viewpoints, we tried to recruit a diverse set of annotators. A total of 22 annotators were recruited who are highly proficient in English and vary in native language, origin and gender, as detailed in Appendix A. This allowed for a balanced gender representation, minimising the possibility for one certain gender to highly influence the annotations.

All annotators were duly informed of the study and their role as annotators, and signed the informed consent form, allowing their annotations to be analysed within the context of this study.

### 4.2 The Annotation Task

The annotation task consisted of two parts. In the first annotation step, the annotators were asked to annotate the associated gender for words in isolation, for each of the 49 individual words (i.e. role names) in an Excel table. They could choose a gender from a pre-defined list (female/male/non-binary) and had the option to select N/A if they really did not associate any gender with the word. For example, annotators had to indicate their gender association for the role name *poet* without any context.

In the second annotation step, given that the aim is to understand how and to what extent context influences the human perception of gender, they annotated the same words presented in a sentence on the annotation platform *Label Studio*[3]. The annotators had to equally indicate from the pre-defined list (female/male/non-binary) which gender they most strongly associated with the word (role name, e.g., *poet* ), but this time in a (gender ambiguous) sentence context, e.g., *Who's the worst poet in Miami?*

## 5 Analysis

In this paper, we focus on a quantitative analysis of selected aspects of the annotations we obtained. We comparatively analysed (1) how an MT system translates a person's gender out-of-context versus in a sentence context, (2) the individual differences between human annotators of gender associations of words out-of-context and in-context, and (3) the comparison of MT with human associations with a focus on gender.

[3]Label Studio `https://labelstud.io/`

| | Human | | MT | |
|---|---|---|---|---|
| | OOC | IC | OOC | IC |
| male | .58 | .58 | .96 | .82 |
| female | .19 | .28 | .04 | .18 |
| Non-binary | .03 | .01 | / | / |
| N/A | .19 | .13 | / | / |

**Table 4:** Label distributions for gender associated with words out-of-context (OOC) and in-context (IC). The label distribution is shown in percentages and was averaged for the human annotators.

### 5.1 Words Out-of-Context vs. In-Context

As shown in Table 4, human annotators associated 58% of the words both out-of- and in-context with the male gender. Furthermore, in the out-of-context scenario, the annotators indicated the words as female for 19% of the cases and did not assign a specific gender (i.e., annotated N/A) also in 19% of cases. When moving to the in-context scenario, the percentage of male-associated words remains the same, but the number of female words increased by 9% and the number of non-binary associations drops minimally (from 3% to 1%). However, the 58% male annotations did not refer to the same words out-of- and in-context. And the N/A labels from out-of-context did not simply change to become female. There was an overall change for which gender was associated with which word, as further explained in the analysis. Interesting to note here is that 19% of the words would not evoke a gender association for human annotators without context, however, annotators are less likely to use the N/A label in-context.

Compared to the human annotations, the MT system shows a clear bias for the male gender, where out-of-context, 96% of words were translated as male. As the MT system does not translate words into gender-inclusive non-binary or 'N/A' genders, the remaining 4% was labeled as female. In-context, the MT system shows less bias, with only 82% of words being translated as male and 18% as female. Overall, the annotation and translation distributions indicate that both MT and human annotators had a tendency towards the male gender, but this bias is much more predominant in the MT system and seems to drop in context.

Clearly depicted in Figure 1, all human annotators often changed the gender annotation for each word from out-of-context to in-context. On average, annotators chose a different associated gender when annotating in-context for 44% (27/60) of

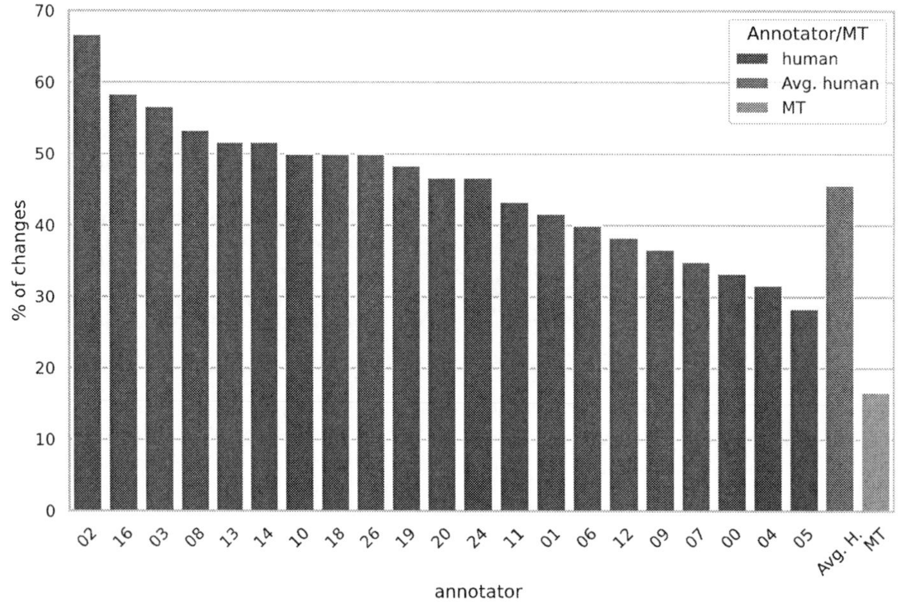


**Figure 1:** Gender changes for words from out-of-context to in-context for (individual and average) annotators and MT

words. In comparison, the MT system only translated a word in context with a different gender for 17% (10/60) of the words. This shows that the MT system predominantly translated each word whether in- or out-of-context in its male generic form, whereas the human association of gender was highly subjective to sentence context. The annotator's association with gender was less consistent for words out-of-context but much more decisive, and also in higher agreement as discussed below, when words were presented in context.

### 5.2 Agreement

For all human annotators, we calculated inter-annotator agreement scores with Fleiss' Kappa (Fleiss, 1971) and Krippendorff's alpha scores (Krippendorff, 2011), which resulted in fair agreement score of 34% and 35% respectively. However, we focus our analysis on an average of the pairwise Cohen's Kappa (Cohen, 1960), to enable averaged pairwise comparison of agreement between the annotators on the one hand, and the annotators versus MT on the other. Since MT-human agreement has to be calculated between each human annotator versus MT and is then averaged across annotators, it made sense to compare agreements this way.

In Table 5, we present the scores for inter-human agreement (human), calculated pairwise, and MT-human agreement on the gender of words in- and out-of-context. These agreement scores, the pairwise Cohen's kappa, indicate fair agreement for in-context labeling and slight agreement for out-of-context labeling both for inter-human and MT-human agreement. Although there are no right or wrong labels, there is a noteworthy increase in agreement for in-context, 18% for inter-human and 15% for MT-human agreement. Notably, inter-human is consistently higher than the agreement between MT and human annotations, despite highly varying annotator profiles. For in-context labeling, inter-human agreement results in an 8% higher agreement than MT-human annotations, and for out-of-context labeling, this results in a 5% higher agreement.

Figure 2 and Figure 3 show the difference between human annotations in and out-of-context, by looking at the percentage of annotators that marked words with the same gender. The x-axes depict the percentage of annotators that agreed on the gender of a word, with a higher percentage, meaning a larger majority. The y-axes depict the number of words that have been agreed on.

Figure 2 shows a relatively equal balance between words that have a small majority (on the left-hand side of the figure) and a strong majority (on

| | | OOC | IC |
|---|---|---|---|
| Human | avg | .18 | .36 |
| | max | .50 | .96 |
| | min | -.13 | .08 |
| | med | .16 | .37 |
| MT-Human | avg | .13 | .28 |
| | max | .37 | .51 |
| | min | -.08 | .04 |
| | med | .11 | .32 |

**Table 5:** Out-of-context (OOC) and in-context (IC) Pairwise Cohen's kappa scores for inter-human and MT-human agreement (including average, minimum, maximum and median for each pair).

the right-hand side of the figure). When comparing these results to Figure 3, which displays the same for in-context labels, this shows us that there are a lot more words with strong agreement (on the right-hand side of the figure).

Table 6 displays the top 10 most agreed-upon words both out-of- and in-context. This shows us that words like *construction worker*, *judge* and *opponent* were annotated with high agreement both in and out-of-context, meaning that annotators had a clearer associated gender for these role names both when seeing the words on their own or when reading the word in a sentence context.

In Table 7, on the other hand, we display the top 10 words with the least agreement in- and out-of-context. These results suggest that words like *baker*, *colleague* and *visitor* were highly ambiguous. Notably, although words like *accountant* and *fighter* have a clear out-of-context associated gender, their in-context annotations have low agreement. The word *fighter* is an interesting example to look at more closely as out-of-context, a decisive 91% of annotators marked the word as male, whereas in-context only 38% of annotators marked the word as male, and the others as female, N/A or non-binary. The sentence this word occurred in was: *It's not the end of the world just yet - I like to think of myself as a fighter and I will keep fighting right until my last run.* This sentence strongly appeals to the individuality of the reader.

We can clearly see here that the human gender association for words is highly dependent on the context that these words are seen in. This phenomenon is much more present in humans than can be seen MT outputs, which predominantly defaults to male.

| out-of-context | in-context |
|---|---|
| construction worker | construction worker |
| judge | judge |
| opponent | opponent |
| dealer | dealer |
| farmer | buddy |
| guard | filmmaker |
| fighter | maestro |
| captain | boss |
| accountant | manager |
| mechanic | student |

**Table 6:** Top 10 most agreed-upon words (over 90% of the votes). With the exception of opponent in-context, all words had *male* as their majority label both in and out-of-context.

| out-of-context | in-context |
|---|---|
| baker | baker |
| colleague | colleague |
| visitor | visitor |
| consumer | salesperson |
| clerk | cook |
| follower | fighter |
| friend | user |
| coordinator | lover |
| musician | accountant |
| designer | dancer |

**Table 7:** Top 10 least agreed-upon words (with majority votes between 33 and 50% of all annotators).

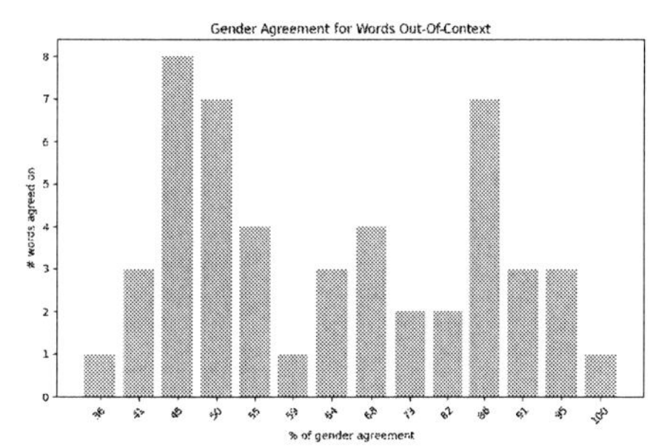


**Figure 2:** Comparison of human annotators' choice of gender for words out-of-context

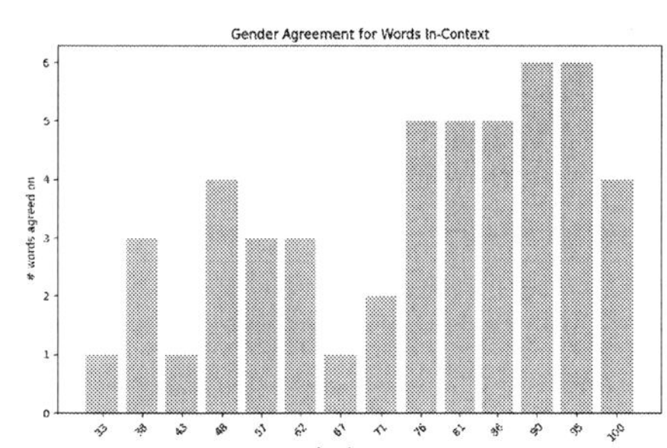


**Figure 3:** Comparison of human annotators' choice of gender for words in-context

## 6 Conclusion

In this paper, we analysed to what extent an MT system translates and humans associate gender with role names both out-of-context and in-context, with no grammatical gender cues in (the source) language.

We note that the MT system is very rigid in its gender translations of role names, primarily translating into generic masculine, particularly for words out-of-context, and seldom changing a role name's gender in certain sentence contexts. Human associations of gender are much more varied, both for words out-of-context and in-context. We particularly see that all annotators have been greatly influenced by the sentence contexts, annotating role names with a gender they associated with that specific context.

The results from this study show that, in comparison to MT, humans have a much more varied understanding of gender and are highly influenced by context. This underlines the diversity and complexity of human associations and gender roles in society and therefore critically highlights the problematic generic masculine translation outputs by MT systems.

The study conducted shows the necessity for continued research to further understand what these diverse human associations for gender in context mean for MT translations. On the one hand, we criticise the generic masculine output of MT systems but on the other hand we see that, for some sentences, the MT does change the gender of role names based on context. This pattern of when and why MT changes gender based on context, and to what extent this relates to human gender associations, will be further studied in the broader research project.

## 7 Limitations and Future Work

A limitation of this exploratory study is that it is only done in a single language direction. Four annotators explicitly noted their mother tongue's influence on their choice of gender annotation for certain words, particularly out-of-context. Many of the annotator's native languages are grammatical gender languages, where role names have a gender assigned. The vast majority of words in grammatical gender languages are traditionally highly influenced by culture and predominantly referred to in the generic masculine.

Two aspects that have been excluded from the analysis of this study but that annotators were asked to annotate were (1) how strongly they associated a word with a specific gender (on a scale of 1-3) and (2) which specific words in the sentence context influenced their choice of gender for the role name in that specific context. Our future research will analyse these aspects and particularly focus on the specific context that influences gender, and relate it to MT. In comparison to analysing influences for human gender associations for words in context, our overarching question that we will focus on is: *What are the triggers that make MT systems change a role name's gender when translating in a specific sentence context?*

## 8 Acknowledgements

This study is part of a broader project, a strategic basic PhD research (1SH5V24N) fully funded by The Research Foundation – Flanders (FWO) for the timespan of four years, from 01.11.2023 until 31.10.2027, and hosted within the Language and Translation Technology Team (LT3) at Ghent University. This research, including the information letter, study guidelines and informed consent form, has been ethically approved by the ethics committee at the Faculty of Arts and Philosophy at Ghent University. The authors would like to thank all annotators for their voluntary and patient annotations, without whom this study could not have been done, and Colin Swaelens and Jasper Degraeuwe for early feedback on the (analysis) of this work.

## 9 Bias Statement

In this paper, we study machine translations of and human associations with gender for role names out-of-context and in-context. The human annotators base their gender associations on language or (stereotypical) cultural and societal knowledge. MT systems predominantly and by default translate role names into the generic masculine, establishing a skewed image of gender in society, thus creating representational harm. Our assumptions are that humans may be stereotyping their assumptions but are nevertheless much more diverse in their overall gender associations for role names, representing a more colourful society, whereas MT systems default to generic masculine but break this pattern for specific and highly stereotypical sentence contexts.

## References


Bolukbasi, Tolga, Kai-Wei Chang, James Zou, Venkatesh Saligrama, and Adam Kalai. 2016. Man is to computer programmer as woman is to homemaker? debiasing word embeddings. In *30th Conference on Neural Information Processing Systems (NIPS 2016)*, Barcelona, Spain.

Caliskan, Aylin, Pimparkar P. Ajay, Tessa Charlesworth, Robert Wolfe, and Mahzarin R. Banaji. 2022. Gender bias in word embeddings: A comprehensive analysis of frequency, syntax, and semantics. In *AAAI/ACM Conference on AI, Ethics, and Society*, page 156–170.

Cohen, Jacob. 1960. A coefficient of agreement for nominal scales. *Educational and psychological measurement*, 20(1):37–46.

Fleiss, Joseph L. 1971. Measuring nominal scale agreement among many raters. *Psychological bulletin*, 76(5):378.

Foundation, Wikimedia. n.d. Wikimedia downloads.

Gygax, Pascal, Ute Gabriel, Oriane Sarrasin, Jane Oakhill, and Alan Garnham. 2008. Generically intended, but specifically interpreted: When beauticians, musicians, and mechanics are all men. In *LANGUAGE AND COGNITIVE PROCESSES*, volume 23:3, pages 464–485.

Hackenbuchner, Janiça, Arda Tezcan, and Joke Daems. forthcoming. Automatic detection of (potential) factors in the source text leading to gender bias in machine translation.

Krippendorff, Klaus. 2011. Computing krippendorff's alpha-reliability. *Computing*, 1:25–2011.

Lardelli, Manuel and Dagmar Gromann. 2023. Gender-fair (machine) translation. In *New Trends in Translation Technology (NeTTT)*, page 166–177, Rhodes Island, Greece.

Lior, Gili and Gabriel Stanovsky. 2023. Comparing humans and models on a similar scale: Towards cognitive gender bias evaluation in coreference resolution. In *Proceedings of the 45th Annual Conference of the Cognitive Science Society*, page 755–762.

McConnell-Ginet, Sally. 2013. Gender and its relation to sex: The myth of 'natural' gender. *In G. G. Corbett (Ed.), The expression of gender. DE GRUYTER.*, page 3–38.

Misersky, Julia, Pascal M. Gygax, Paolo Canal, Ute Gabriel, Alan Garnham, Friederike Braun, Tania Chiarini, Kjellrun Englund, Adriana Hanulikova, Anton Öttl, Jana Valdrova, Lisa Von Stockhausen, and Sabine Sczesny. 2014. Norms on the gender perception of role nouns in czech, english, french, german, italian, norwegian, and slovak. *Behav Res*, 46:841–871.

Mitchell, Tom M. 1980. The need for biases in learning generalizations.

Monti, Johanna. 2020. *Gender issues in machine translation: An unsolved problem?* The Routledge Handbook of Translation, Feminism and Gender.

Raffel, Colin, Noam Shazeer, Adam Roberts, Katherine Lee, Sharan Narang, Michael Matena, Yanqi Zhou, Wei Li, and Peter J. Liu. 2019. Exploring the limits of transfer learning with a unified text-to-text transformer. *arXiv e-prints*.

Saunders, Danielle and Bill Byrne. 2020. Reducing gender bias in neural machine translation as a domain adaptation problem. In *Proceedings of the 58th Annual Meeting of the Association for Computational Linguistics*, page 7724–7736. Association for Computational Linguistics.

Saunders, Danielle, Rosie Sallis, and Bill Byrne. 2021. Neural machine translation doesn't translate gender coreference right unless you make it. In *Proceedings of the Second Workshop on Gender Bias in Natural Language Processing*, page 35–43. Association for Computational Linguistics.

Savoldi, Beatrice, Andrea Piergentili, Dennis Fucci, Matteo Negri, and Luisa Bentivogli. 2024. A prompt response to the demand for automatic gender-neutral translation. In *Proceedings of the 18th Conference of the European Chapter of the Association for Computational Linguistics*, volume 2: Short Papers, page 256–267. Association for Computational Linguistics.

Stahlberg, Dagmar, Friederike Braun, Lisa Irmen, and Sabine Sczesny. 2007. Representation of sexes in the language. In *Social Communication, Frontiers of Social Psychology*, page 163–187, Psychology Press, New York, NY.

Stanovsky, Gabriel, Noah A. Smith, and Luke Zettlemoyer. 2019. Evaluating gender bias in machine translation. In *Proceedings of the 57th Annual Meeting of the Association for Computational Linguistics*, page 1679–1684.

Troles, Jonas-Dario and Ute Schmid. 2021. Extending challenge sets to uncover gender bias in machine translation. impact of stereotypical verbs and adjectives. In *Proceedings of the Sixth Conference on Machine Translation*, page 531–541.

Vanmassenhove, Eva. 2024. Gender bias in machine translation and the era of large language models. *arXiv e-prints*, page 1–24.

## A Appendix: Annotators

**Annotators**

| Gender | Annotators | Country of origin | Mother Tongue |
|---|---|---|---|
| Female | 10 annotators (1 explicitly identifying as trans) | Germany, Belgium, UK, France, The Netherlands, Brazil, Russia | German, Flemish, English, French, Dutch, Portuguese, Russian |
| Male | 10 annotators | Belgium, Turkey, India, UK | Flemish, French, Turkish, Hindi, English |
| Non-binary | 2 annotators | Bulgaria, Belgium | Bulgarian, Flemish |

**Table 8:** List of number of annotators per gender, country of origin and mother tongue.

## B Appendix: Examples

**MT Translation: Gender Change**

| word | sentence |
|---|---|
| friend | After a friend suggested she try it, Ann said, "Sure!" |
| visitor | A health visitor also contacted RBH to raise the issue in July 2020 and an inspection that month found mould in the kitchen, bathroom and a bedroom cupboard needed treatment. |
| therapist | Kensington massage therapist jailed for sexually assaulting clients. |
| musician | In an Instagram video posted last month, the "All Too Well" musician can be seen collaborating with producer Jack Antonoff on the piano. |
| coordinator | One day, she visited a friend who worked as an assistant production coordinator on a set, and she was intrigued by the location department. |
| mechanic | It's important if we want to see a future in which a boy could become a midwife or a girl could become a mechanic. |
| opponent | On Thursday evening, finally, she stepped out onto the court against a top 10 opponent for just the second time of her life. |
| guard | The reserve guard stepped up in the absence of fellow rookie guard Jordan Nixon, who injured her hamstring during warmups. |
| lover | SINGER Matt Goss smooches with his new lover after a dinner date. |

**Table 9:** The MT system translated all words out-of-context (individually) as male, but then as female in the respective sentence context.

**Example Comparison**
MT translations vs. human annotations

| **word**<br>**out-of-context** | **sentence**<br>**in-context** |
|---|---|
| *cook* | I always call myself a cook. |
| MT: male | MT: male |
| Ann: male | Ann: N/A |
| *poet* | Who's the worst poet in Miami? |
| MT: male | MT: male |
| Ann: female | Ann: male |
| *colleague* | Like me, Imogen gets her "dream job" and thinks her life is finally starting - but her confidence and happiness is constantly threatened and undermined by a toxic colleague. |
| MT: male | MT: male |
| Ann: N/A | Ann: female |
| *officer* | I am also the the chief executive officer of Global Women Network, a United Kingdom-based Non-governmental Organisation with roots in Nigeria. |
| MT: male | MT: male |
| Ann: N/A | Ann: female |
| *follower* | I cant even deal with this, one follower wrote alongside two fire emojis, while another wrote: "Love the hair x." |
| MT: male | MT: male |
| Ann: N/A | Ann: female |

**Table 10:** A comparison of a sample of words where the MT system translated the gender of the words differently than the gender association as marked by the human annotators.

**Comparison:** MT gender translations for words in different contexts

| **word**<br>**out-of-context** | **sentence**<br>**in-context** | **MT** |
|---|---|---|
| therapist | Kensington massage therapist jailed for sexually assaulting clients. | female |
| | There are 52 weeks in a year, my therapist continued matter-of-factly, "I know you can't go on a date every single week, but how many do you think you should be going on?" | male |
| clerk | A hotel clerk was caught on video calling a black customer a monkey. | male |
| | The Newark, New Jersey, native was born in 1954 and adopted at age six months out of an orphanage by a township clerk and an auto parts owner. | male |
| lover | SINGER Matt Goss smooches with his new lover after a dinner date. | female |
| | Casual sends a check-in to your friend or lover to see how they're doing or what they're up to. | male |

**Table 11:** Comparison of MT translations of individual words all translated as male out-of-context but then depending on the sentence context, translated the word as either male or female.

# Lost in Translation?
# Approaches to Gender Representation in Multilingual Archives

**Mrinalini Luthra, Brecht Nijman**
GLOBALISE, Huygens Insitute,
Koninklijke Nederlandse Akademie van Wetenschappen (KNAW),
Oudezijds Achterburgwal 185, 1012 DK Amsterdam
{mrinalini.luthra,brecht.nijman}@huygens.knaw.nl

## Abstract

The GLOBALISE project's digitalisation of the Dutch East India Company (VOC) archives raises questions about representing gender and marginalised identities. This paper outlines the challenges of accurately conveying gender information in the archives, highlighting issues such as the lack of self-identified gender descriptions, low representation of marginalised groups, colonial context, and multilingualism in the collection. Machine learning (ML) and machine translation (MT) used in the digitalisation process may amplify existing biases and under-representation. To address these issues, the paper proposes a gender policy for GLOBALISE, offering guidelines and methodologies for handling gender information and increasing the visibility of marginalised identities. The policy contributes to discussions about representing gender and diversity in digital historical research, ML, and MT.

**Disclaimer.** In this paper, words and phrases presented in *"quotation marks and italicised"* are taken from the VOC archives. The records and metadata within these archives contain language and descriptions that are offensive, biased, or distorted. They reflect the prevailing societal attitudes of the VOC, and do not represent our views or those of our institution. Please be aware that engaging with this material may cause distress. We advise approaching the content with care and consideration.



## 1 Introduction

Gender has been the subject of much debate and analysis across various disciplines. In historical archives, gender representation often reflects the biases and power dynamics of the societies that produced them, leading to the marginalisation or erasure of non-normative gender identities. Attempting to describe various genders within historical contexts and across different languages and cultures, while beneficial, often simplifies complexities. Such reductions can inadvertently perpetuate (post)colonial and state-driven narratives of visibility, thus homogenising differences in time, place, and circumstances (Fanon, 1967; Dutta, 2013; Hinchy, 2019).

In parallel, the use of gender as a variable in artificial intelligence (AI) and machine learning (ML) within systems like recommender systems, information retrieval models, and machine translation is growing. However, there is a significant gap in critical analysis on how gender, especially non-binary identities, should be represented, taking into account intersectionality and the racialised nature of gender constructs (Pinney et al., 2023). Addressing gender biases is crucial both in historical archives and AI systems to avoid perpetuating existing inequalities and introducing new biases (Hicks, 2017; Noble, 2018).

The digitalisation (Brennen and Kreiss, 2016) of historical archives, combined with the application of machine learning and machine translation, presents unique challenges and implications for gender representation. This paper uses the GLOBALISE project as a case study to explore these issues. GLOBALISE aims to innovate historical research practices by creating an infrastructure that enables researchers and the public to access



*Proceedings of the 2nd International Workshop on Gender-Inclusive Translation Technologies*, pages 42–55
June 27, 2024 ©2024 European Association for Machine Translation

and explore the Dutch East India Company (VOC) archives, offering insights into the history of colonial expansion and the societies that endured and resisted the VOC's dominance. The project employs both historic and semantic contextualisation, in the form of entity recognition (ER) and event detection (ED), to enrich the archives with additional layers of information (Petram and van Rossum, 2022; Verkijk and Vossen, 2023).

While the primary focus of this paper is on the challenges of accurately representing gender in the context of ML, ER, and ED tasks, the insights gained are particularly relevant for machine translation (MT) as well. The inherently colonial nature of the VOC archives, combined with their complex historical context, the multilingual nature of the documents, and the absence of self-identified gender descriptions, poses significant challenges for accurately translating and representing gender across languages and cultures. Misrepresenting or erasing gender diversity in the translation process can further perpetuate the marginalisation of non-normative identities and distort historical narratives.

This paper thus attempts to answer the question posed in the title "Lost in Translation?" by grappling with the challenges of accurately translating and representing gender diversity across languages and cultures in the multilingual context of the GLOBALISE project and the VOC archives. The question highlights the potential for gender identities and expressions to be misinterpreted, oversimplified, or erased when historical documents are digitised and subjected to machine learning and translation processes. We explore these challenges and propose approaches to mitigate the potential loss or misrepresentation of gender diversity in the digitalisation and translation process.

The remainder of the paper is structured as follows: Section 2 presents a bias statement; Section 3 discusses the use of gender as an analytical variable; Section 4 provides a detailed discussion on the GLOBALISE project, examining the multilingual nature of the archives, gender representation and its challenges within the VOC archives, supplemented by specific examples; Section 5 outlines the first steps toward a gender policy; Section 6 concludes with a discussion on future work and broader implications.

## 2 Bias Statement

VOC archives present a significant challenge for contemporary researchers seeking to uncover the histories of marginalised communities. The vast majority of the records were created by European men employed by the VOC, reflecting their biases, interests, and the prevailing societal attitudes of the time (Wamelen, 2014; Meersbergen, 2017). Searching these records often leads to disappointment due to the violent categorisations of the past, which turned enslaved and colonised people into "nonpersons" (Hartman, 2008; Patterson, 2018; Fuentes, 2016; Zijlstra, 2021). While the colonised population left hardly any self-produced traces, the archive is full of records about them. However, due to the current organisation and accessibility of these archives, the experiences and perspectives of marginalised groups are not only underrepresented but also frequently misrepresented and, in most cases, extremely difficult to access (Trouillot, 2015). Taking from Bowker and Star's (2000) argument in their landmark work "Sorting Things Out: Classifications and their Consequences", the research infrastructures we create have the power to shape and reinforce social categories and power dynamics. As researchers creating an infrastructure to access colonial archives, we must critically examine our own practices to uncover these marginalised histories (Ghosh, 2004; Kars, 2020). Our approach is informed by personal experiences and academic backgrounds, which highlight the limitations and dangers of singular, totalising knowledge systems. This awareness underscores the importance of adopting pluralistic approaches that acknowledge the coexistence of diverse perspectives.

We acknowledge the potential for representational harm (Blodgett et al., 2020) in our work with the VOC archives. Marginalised groups, such as women, non-European actors, and individuals with non-binary genders, and other genders, appear only in traces within these colonial archives, often described by the colonial agents rather than represented in their own voices. This poses significant challenges in correctly attributing gender. The archives' inherent biases and the under-representation of these groups raise concerns that the developed information extraction models may fail to recognise them (under-representation) or attribute incorrect genders (such as stereotyping).

GLOBALISE is considering translating the

archives into various languages, such as Indonesian languages (Bahasa Indonesia, Javanese, Sundanese), Malay, Sinhala, Tamil, and Mandarin, to facilitate increased access. However, this process also carries the risk of perpetuating harm through translation. Misgendering or erasing diverse gender identities in the translated archives can further marginalise these communities and distort historical narratives.

The ramifications of such harms can be far-reaching, particularly for researchers and individuals from communities affected by Dutch colonialism, who may be attempting to write on marginalised histories or seek traces of their ancestors within these archives. Misrepresentation or erasure of their identities and experiences would perpetuate the very harms and marginalisation that these communities have and continue to endure.

## 3 To Gender or Not to Gender?

This section explores the potential benefits and drawbacks of using gender as a variable in the context of the GLOBALISE project and its analysis of the VOC archives, through historical research, machine learning, and machine translation.

### 3.1 Potential Benefits

**1. Revealing Power and Marginalised Histories** Gender is a critical category for understanding power dynamics in historical and cultural contexts. Applying gender as an analytical lens can provide insights into the social, economic, and power dynamics in different societies and time periods (Scott, 1986). Examining gender in conjunction with other identity categories such as race, socio-economic class, and nationality can reveal the complex ways in which power and privilege were and are distributed and experienced in context (Crenshaw, 1991). Focusing on gender can also help uncover the experiences and perspectives of women and other marginalised groups who may have been overlooked in traditional (historical) narratives (Luthra et al., 2023).

**2. Auditing Bias in Machine Learning and Improving Translation** Gender and other demographic variables can be useful to audit biases in machine learning systems. For instance, the incorporation of gender as a variable in ML models can help to uncover and mitigate biases in various domains, such as facial recognition systems, job recommendations, credit scoring, and healthcare (Buolamwini and Gebru, 2018; Omiye et al., 2023; Chen, 2023). Even when gender or other demographic features are not explicitly included in the data, ML models can still discriminate by picking up on proxy factors, as seen in Amazon's hiring algorithm that discriminated against women (Dastin, 2022).

In the field of machine translation, incorporating gender information can help produce more accurate and contextually appropriate translations. For example, in languages with grammatical gender, knowing the gender of the referent can help select the correct pronouns, adjective forms, and other gender-specific linguistic features (Vanmassenhove et al., 2018; Elaraby et al., 2018). Additionally, explicitly modeling gender in machine translation can identify and mitigate gender biases present in training data and algorithms (Saunders et al., 2020; Prates et al., 2020).

### 3.2 Possible Drawbacks

**1. Anachronistic Categories and Limited Sources** Applying modern understandings of gender to historical contexts risks imposing anachronistic categories and obscuring the specific ways in which gender was constructed and experienced in the past (Hartman, 2012). Colonial archives, such as those of the VOC, may not provide sufficient or unbiased information about the (gendered) experiences of all individuals and groups, particularly those who were marginalised or oppressed (Spivak, 1985; Jeurgens and Karabinos, 2020; Hinchy, 2022). Researchers must approach colonial archives critically, recognising their limitations and biases, and seeking to read between the lines and "along and against the grain" to uncover histories of gender (Stoler, 2008).

**2. Reinforcing Binaries and Obscuring Intersectional Identities** Relying solely on gender as a primary analytical category may inadvertently reinforce binary and essentialist notions of gender, failing to capture the diversity and fluidity of gender identities and expressions (Scott, 2010). The Hijra community in South Asia serves as a poignant example of the complexities surrounding gender identity. While sometimes referred to as the "third gender," this term is not without debate, as it risks oversimplifying the multifaceted nature of the Hijra identity. Focusing too heavily on gender alone may obscure other crucial axes of identity that the Hijra community holds dear, such as kinship, religion, class, and embodiment (Reddy, 2005). Moreover, an overemphasis on gender as a variable may also conceal other significant power relations and social categories that shaped the historical context of the VOC, including race, religion, and colonialism (Stoler, 2010). To fully understand the intricacies of identity and power dynamics in the VOC archives, it is essential to adopt an intersectional approach that considers the interplay between gender and other social categories.

**3. Limitations of Machine-Learning and Translation** The use of machine learning techniques to analyse historical documents and archives related to gender in the VOC context poses additional challenges. ML algorithms can perpetuate and amplify biases present in their training data (Noble, 2018; Buolamwini and Gebru, 2018) and may struggle to capture the nuances, ambiguities, and contextual factors crucial for understanding the complexities of gender in historical settings (Jo and Gebru, 2020). Many current approaches to incorporating gender in machine translation rely on binary gender classifications, which may not adequately capture the diversity of gender identities and expressions across cultures and languages (Savoldi et al., 2021; Saunders et al., 2020; Alhafni et al., 2020).

In conclusion, the use of gender as an analytical category in the GLOBALISE project and its analysis of the VOC archives presents both opportunities and challenges. As the project moves forward, it will be crucial to approach the use of gender as a variable with critical reflexivity, acknowledging the limitations and potential drawbacks while also leveraging its potential to uncover new insights and perspectives on the history of the VOC, colonialism, and globalisation.

## 4 Case Study: GLOBALISE

GLOBALISE aims to improve access to the Dutch East India Company archive through the creation of research infrastructure, which will offer an annotated machine-readable version of the *Letters and Papers Received* (OBP) section of VOC archives.[1] The OBP consists of the documents that the Dutch offices of the company received from its offices in its region of operation which ranged from the South African Cape to Japan.

The GLOBALISE project team consists of two main groups: historians who collect and curate reference data related to the collection, and a team responsible for training language models for entity recognition (ER) and event detection (ED). The entities identified in the archives will be linked to the curated reference data as well as existing reference vocabularies. Furthermore, the annotations will be interconnected to provide additional context for future users of the GLOBALISE research infrastructure. The annotators creating the ground truth data for the ER and ED models are from within the project team, ensuring a close collaboration between the historical and computational aspects of the project. This structure allows for a multidisciplinary approach to the digitalisation and enrichment of the VOC archives, leveraging the expertise of historians and computational linguists to create a comprehensive and accessible research resource. By providing annotated and contextualised data, the GLOBALISE project aims to facilitate new insights into the history of the VOC and its impact on the regions under its influence.

### 4.1 The Corpus

The OBP consists of approximately 5 million scans of handwritten material, making up 1,042,989,589 tokens.[2] It consists of a wide variety of documents, including but not limited to internal and external correspondence, resolutions, court cases, censuses, and summarising reports tying these together called the General Letters. TThe majority of these documents were written in Dutch by European men employed by the company (Meersbergen, 2017). Nevertheless, the archive is seeped through with languages other than Dutch, including many local non-European languages. In addition to a small series of letters sent over in their original language and a more substantial series of such letters in translation (±5% of documents)[3], the Dutch of the archive is laden with

[1] `https://globalise.huygens.knaw.nl`

[2] The most recent version of transcriptions can be accessed here: `https://transcriptions.globalise.huygens.knaw.nl/`. The whole corpus can also be downloaded at: `https://hdl.handle.net/10622/LVXSBW`.

[3] This is five percent of documents, not five percent of the corpus, and consists of 8214 documents marked as "Translaat" (translation) within the "Indigenous correspondence" section of the "Towards a New Age of Partnership" (TANAP) index of the OBP. This is by no means an exhaustive list of translations in the archive. Translated documents do not always carry "translation" in their title. Additionally translation appears in other forms as well.

a vocabulary originating from the languages of the region (Pepping, 2024).

### 4.2 Gender in the Corpus

Gender is rarely self-identified in the VOC archives and is usually assigned by third parties, such as scribes and translators, often in reductive and incorrect ways. This poses challenges for accurately representing gender in the GLOBALISE project, as the information reflects the assumptions and biases of the record creators rather than the lived experiences and identities of the individuals described. The lack of historical and cultural context further complicates the interpretation of gender, as the concepts of sex and gender may not have been distinguished by the Europeans writing these records.[4]

Nevertheless, some traces of gender identities outside the historical Western binary categorisations are found in the archives. Given these traces and challenges of self-identification, gender in the GLOBALISE project is taken as a construct encompassing both sex and gender, given that in most cases they are conflated and indistinguishable, and are mostly not based on self-identification but based on the assumptions of the writers of the archives. Moreover, care must be taken not to flatten these identities when approaching them through modern Western concepts of gender. Many of these identities had intrinsic relations to sacredness, positions at court or spiritual roles, and connections to social status and enslavement (Arvas, 2019; Andaya, 2018; Bowie, 2023; Hinchy, 2022; Ismoyo, 2020; Peletz, 2009).

#### 4.2.1 Explicit Gender Indicators

| term (Dutch) | term (English) | count |
|---|---|---|
| bisoe — bisoes — bissoe — bissoes | *bissu* | 34 |
| sida sida | *sida sida* | 0 |
| hijra — hisra | hijra | 1 |
| besnedene | "castrated" | 152 |
| eunuch — eunich | eunuch | 65 |

**Table 1:** Occurrence of selected terms describing individuals outside the gender binary.

The most explicit form of gendering in the archive occurs where people are explicitly described as belonging to a particular gender (See Tables 2 and 1). This is most often a form of "man" or "woman" (see example (1)). Although mentions of genders outside the binary are very rare, they are sometimes explicitly referenced, though this does not necessarily mean they are acknowledged as distinct gender identities. Example (2) shows a case where *bissu*, one of the Bugis genders, are explicitly mentioned (Ismoyo, 2020). While the *Bissu* in this passage are described as distinct from men or women, they are still misgendered as *"men"* within the passage and their identity is conflated with sexual practice (*"knowledge"* in this case refers to sexual intercourse). In other cases, these identities are even further obscured, either by being grouped together into catch-all categories describing gendered or sexual "otherness", such as *"Eunuch"*, *"hermafrodiet"* (*"hermaphrodite"*), or *"besnedene"* (*"castrate"*), or by simply being subsumed into binary categorisations (Andaya, 2018; Gannon, 2011; Hinchy, 2017). As Table 1 shows, these terms are relatively more common compared to in-community terms such as *bissu* or *hijra*. Both are very rare compared to terms referencing binary gender (Table 2). Additionally, these gender identities may be described only through another one of their identity axes, for instance solely as "priests".

(1) *6: **manspersoonen** ende een hollantsche **vrouw***[5]

6: **man** persons and a Hollandish **woman**

(2) *Buijten nog eenige sleep van ruijm 200. Coppen zoo **mans** als **vrouwen** die haar in de [z]aal en buijten op de stoep nedersette[,] ongerekent nog 20. **bissoes** of zoo genaamde mannen die de bekenning der vrouwen zouden hebben afgeswooren* [6]

Outside some more followers, roughly 200 heads, **men** as well as **women**, who waited in the hall as well as outside on the street, uncounted another 20 **bissu** or so-called men who have sworn off the knowledge of women.[7]

[4]This is further complicated by the fact that both sex and gender are socially constructed (Browne, 2010).

[5]National Archives (NA), the Hague, Archive of the Verenigde Oost-Indische Compagnie (VOC), 1.04.02, inventory number 1121, p. 833, https://transcriptions.globalise.huygens.knaw.nl/detail/urn:globalise:NL-HaNA_1.04.02_1121_0060

[6]NA, VOC, 8194, fo. 205. https://transcriptions.globalise.huygens.knaw.nl/detail/urn:globalise:NL-HaNA_1.04.02_8194_0213

[7]NA, VOC, 8194, fo. 205r. https://transcriptions.globalise.huygens.knaw.

| term (English) | masculine term (Dutch) | count | feminine term (Dutch) | count |
|---|---|---|---|---|
| person | mansper* | 1548 | vrouwsper* | 1642 |
| “man slave” / “woman slave” | mansla*f — manslav* | 3450 | vrouwsla*f — vrouwslav* | 69 |
| “slave” | sla*f — slav* | 167114 | slavin* | 25358 |
| farmer | boer | 3230 | boerin | 67 |
| *encik* | intje | 13589 | – | – |
| *njai* | – | – | njaij — njeij | 601 |
| widow(er) | weduwna*r | 20 | weduwe | 22099 |
| son / daughter | zoon — soon | 79659 | dogter — dochter — doghter | 19266 |
| king / queen | koning — coning — coninck | 304109 | koningin — coningin | 3407 |

**Table 2:** Occurrence of selected gendered terms.

### 4.2.2 Personal Nouns as Gender Indicators

As Dutch is a grammatical gender language, the archive is in no shortage of explicit gender-markers. Personal nouns in particular carry potentially valuable information on (perceived) social gender. A term’s grammatical gender does not always coincide with the social gender associated with it. For instance, *“wijf”*, (wife or woman) is grammatically neuter, but socially feminine. However, in the majority of cases grammatical and social gender of personal nouns in Dutch align. See for instance example (3)).

(3) *“12 **boeren** en **boerinnen**”*.[8]
12 **farmers**$_M$ and **farmers**$_F$

This approach also carries a number of pitfalls. First, following on from the previous point, these forms make it nearly impossible to recognise any gender that falls outside the man–woman binary. Second, commonly occurring issues regarding gender in language, such as masculine generics (see example (4)) and marked femaleness (see example (5)), also complicate this strategy. As Stahlberg et al. (2007) point out, it cannot be generally assumed that by using the masculine, particularly the masculine plural, the author considered an individual to be a man (let alone how that individual identified). At the same time, annotating only non-masculine terms reinforces the “othering” of women and genders beyond the binary. Finally, as mentioned, a small but non-negligible number of documents are translations of documents received in other languages (this does not include translations of spoken accounts or summaries of in-person interactions in other languages). Many of these are translations from genderless languages such as Malay or Javanese, and gender may have been introduced in the process of translation.

(4) *“de principaalste **actrice** van deese **gaauwdieven** troep”*.[9]
the principal **actress** of this gang of **thieves**$_M$.

(5) *“en Conting groot 15. Coij[ang]s bem[an]t met 8. chineesen en 12. javanen waeronder een **vrouwspersoon**”*.[10]
a kunting, large 15 koj[ang]s, manned by 8 chinese and 12 javanese including a **woman** person.

### 4.2.3 Loan Words as Gender Indicators

Loanwords are words adopted from one language into another without translation, often as a result of cultural contact or influence (Durkin, 2014). In colonial archives, loanwords originate from interactions between colonisers and indigenous populations, serving to facilitate communi-

nl/detail/urn:globalise:NL-HaNA_1.04.02_8194_0213

[8]NA, VOC, 4074, fo. 16r, https://transcriptions.globalise.huygens.knaw.nl/detail/urn:globalise:NL-HaNA_1.04.02_4074_0022.

[9]NA, VOC, 10936, https://transcriptions.globalise.huygens.knaw.nl/detail/urn:globalise:NL-HaNA_1.04.02_10936_0243.

[10]NA, VOC, 1945, 75, https://transcriptions.globalise.huygens.knaw.nl/detail/urn:globalise:NL-HaNA_1.04.02_1945_0086.

cation and reflect the integration of indigenous systems into colonial structures. They offer insights into cultural exchange, administrative integration, and power dynamics within colonial societies (Naregal, 1999; Cohn, 1996). For instance, "Baboe", from Javanese and Malay (also spelled as "babu") originally referred to a female servant or domestic worker in Southeast Asian societies. In Dutch colonial households, "baboes" were often employed to perform domestic chores and childcare duties for Dutch families. The use of this term in colonial archives highlights the hierarchical relationship between Dutch employers and indigenous domestic workers, reflecting the social stratification based on race and class in colonial society.[11] Moreover, many of the gendered identities in the VOC archives such as "bissu" are also loanwords.

Loanwords, particularly those used as terms of address, titles, and professions, constitute the final group of gender indicators to consider in the archive. Not considering loanwords while considering gendered words in Dutch would result in a disparity between the gendering of indigenous individuals and Europeans in the corpus. Furthermore, one could argue that these terms are more likely to reflect personal identity, though they may still be assigned from within the same language group. A particular pitfall with these terms is that they tend not to be recognised, even by human annotators, often being identified as parts of names. Identifying gendered loanwords can be particularly difficult due to several factors. Firstly, they originate from hundreds of languages throughout the region. Secondly, they are often poorly transliterated using Early Modern Dutch spelling, at times rendering them unrecognisable even to (native) speakers. For instance "Encik" (Mr. in Malay) is commonly written as "Intje" in the corpus. Lastly, successful identification of gendered loanwords is limited further where languages which have become endangered or even extinct, oftentimes in direct result to violence enacted by the VOC (Pepping, 2024). Additionally, care should be taken not to introduce gender to titles which do not explicitly carry it. Many forms of address might say more about class, caste, race or closeness than they do about gender (Yusra et al., 2023). Historically, gender neutral titles have been glossed in explicitly gendered ways.

Note that names have not been listed as a gender indicator in this section. Names are dubious carriers of gender in any context, and only more so in a multilingual one (Das and Paik, 2021; Saunders and Olsen, 2023). The same name may have very different associations across languages. Additionally, the Early Modern Dutch transliterations of names may render them indistinguishable or unrecognisable.

## 5 Developing a Gender Policy for GLOBALISE

GLOBALISE aims to develop a gender policy that respectfully represents the diversity of gender identities and experiences within the VOC archives. This policy will serve as a framework for addressing the challenges and limitations of working with historical sources, where gender information may be incomplete, biased, or absent. The gender policy will guide the project's approaches to data collection, annotation, analysis, and interpretation, ensuring that the resulting research infrastructure is sensitive to the complexities of gender across different historical and cultural contexts.

**Principles of the GLOBALISE gender policy** include:

1. Recognise the historical and cultural specificity of gender categories and expressions
2. Acknowledge the limitations and biases inherent in historical sources, particularly those created within colonial contexts
3. Strive to represent gender diversity in a manner that is respectful, accurate, and inclusive
4. Engage with relevant communities, scholars, and stakeholders to inform the development and implementation of the policy
5. Ensure transparency and accountability in the project's handling of gender-related information

The remaining section outlines guidelines and strategies for handling gender-related information in the GLOBALISE project.

[11] Note: It's worth acknowledging that some of these loanwords have become fully integrated into the colonial language itself, reflecting the enduring influence of colonial interactions on linguistic evolution. For instance, words like "loot" (derived from the Hindi word "lut") meaning "plunder" and "jungle" (originating from the Hindi word meaning "dense forest") are now commonplace in English vocabulary, serving as reminders of the historical connections between colonial past and contemporary language usage.

## 5.1 Polyvocal Gender Vocabulary

To address the diverse gender identities in the VOC archives, as discussed in section 4, GLOBALISE adopts a "polyvocal gender vocabulary" (Peletz, 2009). This approach allows for the inclusion of multiple gender classifications within a single knowledge organisation system (Tudhope and Lykke Nielsen, 2006; Hjørland and Gnoli, 2016), enabling the representation of historical and cultural specificities of gender. By employing this method, GLOBALISE aims to avoid imposing anachronistic or Western-centric categories onto the historical records while making gender diversity visible and searchable. The project seeks to represent gender categories from various cultures on their own terms, rather than "being through others" (Fanon, 1967).

The polyvocal gender vocabulary draws on the concept of "polyvocality" or "polyphony" (Bakhtin, 1984), which is a narrative feature that emphasises the simultaneous inclusion of multiple voices and perspectives. This approach aligns with the concept of "practical ontology" developed in anthropology and science and technology studies (STS), which recognises the coexistence of multiple, culturally-specific ways of understanding and categorising the world (Gad et al., 2015; Barth, 1993; Geertz, 1973). By adopting a polyvocal gender vocabulary, GLOBALISE aims to represent the diverse and "situated" (Haraway, 2016) understandings of gender present in the VOC archives, while acknowledging the challenges and limitations of working across multiple cultural and historical contexts.

### 5.1.1 Detecting Gendered Terms and Constructing a Polyvocal Gender Vocabulary

To address the challenges of detecting gendered terms in the VOC archives, GLOBALISE will employ an iterative process involving vocabulary development, manual annotation, and machine learning, as illustrated in Figure 1.

**Gender Classification** The project will adopt a four-level hierarchy with the following top-level categories: M (man), W (woman), U (undefined, cannot infer gender information from the text), and O (other gender categories). The "O" category, an intermediate step, will be further subdivided manually into more specific gender identities based on

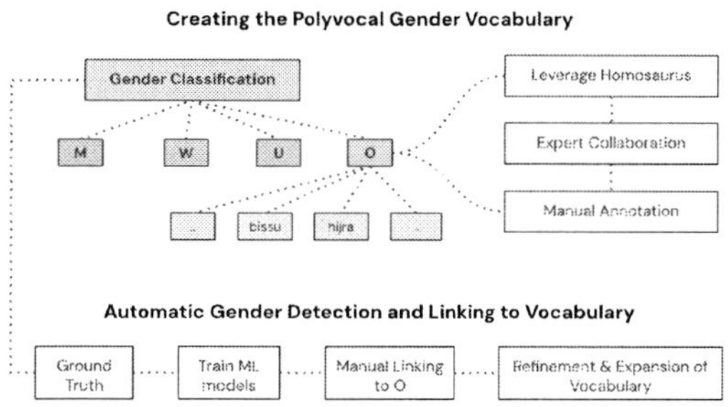


**Figure 1:** Creating the Polyvocal Gender Vocabulary and Automatic Gender Detection

the expertise of historians and cultural experts, allowing for granular representation while ensuring the machine learning models will not ignore and misrepresent and misclassify these other gender categories. This decision is based on our experience that marginalised groups are mentioned in the VOC archives but only in low frequencies and often with wrong and insufficient contextual information.[12]

**Creating the Gender Vocabulary** The gender vocabulary will be developed through an iterative process involving the use of existing linked data vocabularies, collaboration with experts, and manual annotation.

1. **Leverage the Homosaurus**: GLOBALISE will leverage existing vocabularies such as the Homosaurus (Homosaurus Editorial Board, 2019), a linked data vocabulary of LGBTQ+ terms developed for cultural heritage institutions, as a starting point. While the Homosaurus focuses on modern terminology, its principles of providing a standardised yet inclusive ontology for gender diversity will inform the development of GLOBALISE's gender vocabulary. However, the project will adapt these principles to address the specific challenges posed by the VOC archives, such as the lack of self-identified gender information and the presence of historical terms and categories that may not map neatly onto contemporary understandings of gender.[13]

2. **Collaborate with Experts**: GLOBALISE

[12]So far, we have only found about 5 instances of the "bissu" in the archives and their descriptions in the archive are reductive and incorrect.

[13]Terms like "Hijra" and "bissu" are present in the Homosaurus and can be used to check their presence in the GLOBALISE corpus.

will work with gender scholars, communities and individuals from different gender groups, and historians specialising in regions covered by the VOC to create, refine, and expand the gender vocabulary. These experts will help identify culturally-specific gender terms and categories relevant to the historical context of the VOC archives and the early modern "Indian Ocean world".

3. **Manual annotation and Iterative Refinement**: Using the initial gender vocabulary, annotators will manually label a subset of the VOC archives with gender information, employing the hierarchical gender classification scheme defined earlier. During the annotation process, new gendered terms are expected to be identified and added to the vocabulary.[14] This requires that annotators have the relevant linguistic background to recognise these terms.[15]

**Automatic Gender and Linking to Gender Vocabulary** With the manually annotated dataset serving as the ground truth, GLOBALISE will employ automatic gender detection using machine learning models to identify gendered terms at scale in the VOC archives, as illustrated in Figure 1.

1. **Training machine learning models**: The manually annotated dataset will be used to train machine learning models, such as entity recognition systems (Ehrmann et al., 2023), to automatically detect gendered terms in the larger corpus. The machine learning models will assign one of the four top-level gender categories (M, W, U, or O) to each detected gendered term.

2. **Applying the models to the full corpus**: The trained machine learning models will be applied to the entire VOC archive to automatically detect and classify gendered terms at scale.

3. **Manual linking to specific categories**: After the automatic gender detection process, the gendered terms classified as "O" will be examined and manually linked to more specific gender categories in the gender vocabulary by GLOBALISE's researchers, experts, and community members. This manual linking process allows for a more granular representation of non-binary and culturally-specific gender identities while ensuring that the machine learning models do not overlook these categories. Moreover, this step allows us to audit the outputs of the machine learning models to avoid misgendering (Kotek et al., 2023; Bender et al., 2021; Hamidi et al., 2018), especially given that descriptions that follow or precede gendered terms in the VOC archives, are often incorrect or reductive as explained in the example of "bissu" in subsection 4.2.

4. **Iterative refinement**: As new gendered terms are discovered during the automatic gender detection and manual linking processes, they will be incorporated into the gender vocabulary and used to refine the machine learning models. This iterative refinement ensures that the polyvocal gender vocabulary remains accurate, comprehensive, and culturally sensitive.

### 5.2 Gendered "Loanwords", and their Translations

As discussed in Section 4.2.3 on loanwords, GLOBALISE will pay close attention to the presence of loanwords in the corpus. Annotators will be trained in detecting loanwords, and the project will benefit from annotators of diverse cultural and historical backgrounds as well as insights from local communities and experts. Additionally, the project will investigate the use of multilingual models such as BERT (2018) and translation technologies to automatically detect loanwords in the VOC archives (Nath et al., 2022).

Recent research has emphasised the importance of considering gender diversity in machine translation, as neural machine translation systems often perpetuate gender biases and fail to accurately translate gender-neutral or non-binary language (Vanmassenhove et al., 2018; Savoldi et al., 2021). By developing a "polyvocal gender vocabulary," GLOBALISE can contribute to more gender- and culturally-sensitive machine translation by introducing contextual aspects of gender.

However, when translating the VOC archives, the project must also consider the presence of gen-

[14] Also based on our experience developing reference data on commodities in the GLOBALISE project (Pepping et al., 2023).

[15] Annotators without such knowledge are more likely to mistake gendered loanwords as names or (merely) professions.

dered loanwords, which reflect the complex linguistic and cultural dynamics of the colonial encounter. These loanwords often carry the "hierarchies of power" (Naregal, 1999) that characterized colonial bilingualism, and simply translating them into other languages risks overwriting or erasing important historical and cultural nuances. To address this issue, the GLOBALISE project's initial strategy will be to preserve gendered loanwords in their original form when translating the VOC archives into other languages. By retaining these loanwords, the project aims to maintain the visibility of the complex cultural and linguistic exchanges that took place in early modern history while providing context and explanations to help readers understand their meanings and connotations.

### 5.3 Gender Identification

As discussed in subsection 4.2, GLOBALISE treats gender as a complex construct encompassing both sex and gender, which are often conflated and indistinguishable in third-person historical records without self-identification.

**Avoiding Gender Assignment Based on Names** The project avoids assigning gender based solely on names as this can introduce biases (Luthra et al., 2023) and unwarranted assumptions about individuals' identities (Savoldi et al., 2021), especially for non European cultures, beyond that was already done in the creation of the records (Das and Paik, 2021). Instead, the project will rely on explicit references to gender or contextual "trigger words" (Ehrmann et al., 2023), such as titles, roles, and gendered nouns, to infer gender when possible. These include terms such as koningin" (queen), sultana," mevrouw" (madam), meneer" (sir), radja" (king), rani" (queen), coopvrouw" (merchant woman), priesteressen" (priestesses), "weduwe" (widow), "slavinne" (female slave), "capados", eunuch", and "bissu."

However, the project acknowledges that these references often reflect the assumptions and biases of the record creators rather than the self-identified gender of the individuals described. A not very straightforward example of this is the case of Matthias Panholsser, with a stereotypical Dutch male name, one of 52 persons in the VOC Opvarenden[16] [VOC Sailors], who was dismissed on the grounds of being a "vrouw" (woman). Here, we do not want to conclude that Matthias was a trans-man at the risk of "trans-ing" history (Hinchy, 2022). Perhaps Matthias only disguised as a man to serve on the VOC ships, looking for better economic opportunities. But of this we cannot know, due to the insufficient information, and thus adding our own interpretation. We return to the case of Matthias breifly in 5.4.

**Handling Grammatical Gender in Dutch** As Dutch is a grammatical gender language, personal nouns can offer valuable perceived gender information. However, the project will be mindful of the pitfalls associated with grammatical gender, such as masculine generics potentially obscuring women and non-binary individuals, and the "othering" reinforced by only annotating non-masculine terms (Stahlberg et al., 2007), as discussed in examples (4) and (5).

### 5.4 Modeling Gender Fluidity

Gender reassignments and gender fluidity have existed throughout history, as exemplified by the Hijras in South Asia (Hinchy, 2022; Reddy, 2005). However, current systems for classifying gender often fail to capture this reality, employing static categorisations that inadequately represent how individuals' genders can shift over their lifetimes (Andrews et al., 2024). Recognising this limitation, the GLOBALISE project aims to develop methods for modeling gender fluidity within the VOC archives to better represent changes in gender identity over time.

One approach is to use event-based modeling, where gender is treated as a temporal attribute that can change at specific points in an individual's life. This allows for the representation of gender transitions and the evolution of an individual's gender identity (Andrews et al., 2024). By employing event-based modeling, the project can capture pivotal moments when an individual's expressed or documented gender may have shifted, potentially due to societal pressures, personal needs, or changing circumstances. While the archival records may only provide a limited, biased glimpse into an individual's gender experience, modeling gender fluidity as a series of events acknowledges the possibility of more complex gender journeys than what is immediately apparent. This way, the project can

[16] https://www.nationaalarchief.nl/onderzoeken/index/nt00444/cc19411e-c864-11e6-9d8b-00505693001d

shed light on the diverse gender expressions, nonconformities, and transgressions (for instance the case of Matthias Panholsser who was dismissed for "being a woman") that have existed throughout history (Nationaal Archief, nd).

### 5.5 Evaluation and Intersectionality

To ensure the accuracy and fairness of the gender vocabulary and detection methods, GLOBALISE will conduct regular evaluations and audits. One important aspect of this evaluation is studying bias along intersectional axes, such as race, ethnicity, and gender (Haim et al., 2024). By examining the interactions between these different dimensions of identity, the project can identify and mitigate potential biases in the gender classification and detection systems. The evaluation process will involve collaboration with experts in gender studies, history, and cultural heritage, as well as members of affected communities.

## 6 Conclusion, Discussions, Future Work

This paper encapsulates the central challenges we face in the GLOBALISE project in attempting to accurately representing and translating the diverse gender identities and expressions found within the multilingual VOC archives. Through this work, we aim to contribute to the broader discussion on the challenges of detecting gender at scale in multilingual and multicultural corpora. This paper has outlined the problems in our endeavor and proposed strategies to address them, grappling with the complex issues of navigating linguistic and cultural boundaries while striving for respectful and useful representations.

These challenges are not unique to GLOBALISE; they apply to those working in digital humanities and those working with socially constructed data in fields like machine learning and machine translation. Representing gender diversity across historical, linguistic, and cultural contexts in a culturally sensitive and computationally feasible manner is a broader issue that requires ongoing exploration and dialogue. We hope that this paper can contribute to informing and advancing these broader discussions and practices around the representation of gender diversity. As we continue to develop and refine our methods for representing gender diversity in the GLOBALISE project, we welcome input and collaboration from researchers and communities working on similar challenges in other domains.

In terms of future work, the GLOBALISE project will start with the creation of the polyvocal gender vocabulary and initial attempts at gender detection in the VOC archives. We plan to collaborate with area studies specialists to think about gender from the various regions once under the VOC empire, ensuring that our approaches are culturally informed and sensitive to the specific historical and linguistic contexts of the archives.

**Acknowledgements:** This publication is part of the project GLOBALISE (with project number 175.2019.003) of the Research Infrastructure research program financed by the Dutch Research Council (NWO). We extend our gratitude to the entire GLOBALISE team, with special thanks to the historical contextualisation team for their insightful discussions on gender classifications and their consequences. We would also like to express our appreciation to Sofia Coppola who inspired the title of this article with her most excellent film. Finally, we extend our appreciation to Kevin, Asawari, Julia, and Lolo for their invaluable support throughout the process.

## References

Alhafni, Bashar, Nizar Habash, and Houda Bouamor. 2020. Gender-aware reinflection using linguistically enhanced neural models. In Costa-jussà, Marta R., Christian Hardmeier, Will Radford, and Kellie Webster, editors, *Proceedings of the Second Workshop on Gender Bias in Natural Language Processing*, pages 139–150, Barcelona, Spain (Online), December. Association for Computational Linguistics.

Andaya, Leonard Y. 2018. The *Bissu*: Study of a third gender in indonesia. In Zamfira, Andreea, Christian de Montlibert, and Daniela Radu, editors, *Gender in Focus: Identities, Codes, Stereotypes and Politics*, pages 62–87. Barbara Budrich, Opladen, German.

Andrews, Tara L, Marius Deierl, and Carla Ebel. 2024. Gender Assignment as an Event—a Contemporary Approach for the Adequate Depiction of Historical Gender Categories. *Digital Scholarship in the Humanities*, 39(1):5–12.

Arvas, Abdulhamit. 2019. Early modern eunuchs and the transing of gender and race. *Journal for Early Modern Cultural Studies*, 19(4):116–136.

Bakhtin, Mikhail. 1984. *Problems of Dostoevsky's poetics*. University of Minnesota Press, Minneapolis, Minnesota, United States.

Barth, Fredrik. 1993. *Balinese worlds*. University of Chicago Press, Chicago, Illnois, United States.

Bender, Emily M, Timnit Gebru, Angelina McMillan-Major, and Shmargaret Shmitchell. 2021. On the dangers of stochastic parrots: Can language models be too big? In *Proceedings of the 2021 ACM conference on fairness, accountability, and transparency*, pages 610–623.

Blodgett, Su Lin, Solon Barocas, Hal Daumé III, and Hanna Wallach. 2020. Language (technology) is power: A critical survey of "bias" in NLP. In Jurafsky, Dan, Joyce Chai, Natalie Schluter, and Joel Tetreault, editors, *Proceedings of the 58th Annual Meeting of the Association for Computational Linguistics*, pages 5454–5476, Online, July. Association for Computational Linguistics.

Bowie, Katherine A. 2023. Eunuchs in burmese history: An overview. *Journal of Southeast Asian Studies*, 54(4):621–644.

Bowker, Geoffrey C and Susan Leigh Star. 2000. *Sorting things out: Classification and its consequences*. MIT press.

Brennen, J Scott and Daniel Kreiss. 2016. Digitalization. *The international encyclopedia of communication theory and philosophy*, pages 1–11.

Browne, Simone. 2010. Digital epidermalization: Race, identity and biometrics. *Critical Sociology*, 36(1):131–150.

Buolamwini, Joy and Timnit Gebru. 2018. Gender shades: Intersectional accuracy disparities in commercial gender classification. In *Conference on fairness, accountability and transparency*, pages 77–91. PMLR.

Chen, Zhisheng. 2023. Ethics and discrimination in artificial intelligence-enabled recruitment practices. *Humanities and Social Sciences Communications*, 10(1):567, September.

Cohn, Bernard S. 1996. *Colonialism and Its Forms of Knowledge*. Princeton University Press, Princeton, NJ.

Crenshaw, Kimberle. 1991. Mapping the margins: Intersectionality, identity politics, and violence against women of color. *Stanford Law Review*, 43(6):1241–1299.

Das, Sudeshna and Jiaul H Paik. 2021. Context-sensitive gender inference of named entities in text. *Information Processing & Management*, 58(1):102423.

Dastin, Jeffrey. 2022. Amazon Scraps Secret AI Recruiting Tool that Showed Bias against Women. In Martin, Kirsten, editor, *Ethics of Data and Analytics*. Auerbach Publications, Boca Raton, Florida, United States. Num Pages: 4.

Devlin, Jacob, Ming-Wei Chang, Kenton Lee, and Kristina Toutanova. 2018. Bert: Pre-training of deep bidirectional transformers for language understanding. *arXiv preprint arXiv:1810.04805*.

Durkin, Philip. 2014. *Borrowed Words: A History of Loanwords in English*. Oxford University Press, January.

Dutta, Aniruddha, 2013. *An Epistemology of Collusion: Hijras, Kothis and the Historical (Dis) Continuity of Gender/Sexual Identities in Eastern India*, chapter 14, pages 305–329. John Wiley & Sons, Ltd.

Ehrmann, Maud, Ahmed Hamdi, Elvys Linhares Pontes, Matteo Romanello, and Antoine Doucet. 2023. Named entity recognition and classification in historical documents: A survey. *ACM Computing Surveys*, 56(2):1–47.

Elaraby, Mostafa, Ahmed Y. Tawfik, Mahmoud Khaled, Hany Hassan, and Aly Osama. 2018. Gender aware spoken language translation applied to english-arabic. In *2018 2nd International Conference on Natural Language and Speech Processing (ICNLSP)*, pages 1–6.

Fanon, Frantz. 1967. *Black skin, white masks*. Grove Press, New York.

Fuentes, Marisa J. 2016. *Dispossessed lives: Enslaved women, violence, and the archive*. University of Pennsylvania Press.

Gad, Christopher, Casper Bruun Jensen, and Brit Ross Winthereik. 2015. Practical Ontology: Worlds in STS and anthropology. *NatureCulture*, (3):67–86.

Gannon, Shane. 2011. Exclusion as language and the language of exclusion: Tracing regimes of gender through linguistic representations of the "eunuch". *Journal of the History of Sexuality*, 20(1):1–27.

Geertz, Clifford. 1973. *The interpretation of cultures*. Basic books, New York City, New York, United States.

Ghosh, Durba. 2004. Decoding the nameless: gender, subjectivity, and historical methodologies in reading the archives of colonial india. *A New Imperial History: Culture, Identity, and Modernity in Britain and the Empire*, pages 1660–1840.

Haim, Amit, Alejandro Salinas, and Julian Nyarko. 2024. What's in a name? auditing large language models for race and gender bias.

Hamidi, Foad, Morgan Klaus Scheuerman, and Stacy M. Branham. 2018. Gender recognition or gender reductionism? the social implications of embedded gender recognition systems. In *Proceedings of the 2018 CHI Conference on Human Factors in Computing Systems*, CHI '18, page 1–13, New York, NY, USA. Association for Computing Machinery.

Haraway, Donna. 2016. 'situated knowledges: The science question in feminism and the privilege of partial perspective'. In *Space, gender, knowledge: Feminist readings*, pages 53–72. Routledge, London, United Kingdom.

Hartman, Saidiya. 2008. Venus in two acts. *Small Axe: A Caribbean Journal of Criticism*, 12(2):1–14.

Hartman, Saidiya. 2012. The time of slavery. In *Enchantments of Modernity*, pages 447–468. Routledge India.

Hicks, Mar. 2017. *Programmed inequality: How Britain discarded women technologists and lost its edge in computing*. MIT press, Cambridge, Massachusetts, United States.

Hinchy, Jessica. 2017. The eunuch archive: Colonial records of non-normative gender and sexuality in india. *Culture, Theory and Critique*, 58(2):127–146.

Hinchy, Jessica. 2019. *Governing Gender and Sexuality in Colonial India: The Hijra, c.1850–1900*. Cambridge University Press.

Hinchy, Jessica Bridgette. 2022. Hijras and south asian historiography. *History Compass*, 20(1):e12706.

Hjørland, Birger and Claudio Gnoli. 2016. Isko encyclopedia of knowledge organization.

Homosaurus Editorial Board. 2019. Homosaurus: An international lgbtq linked data vocabulary. `http://homosaurus.org/`.

Ismoyo, Petsy Jessy. 2020. Decolonising gender identities in Indonesia: A study of bissue 'the trans-religious leader' in bugis people. *Paradigma: Jurnal Kajian Budaya*, 10(3):277–288.

Jeurgens, Charles and Michael Karabinos. 2020. Paradoxes of curating colonial memory. *Archival Science*, 20(3):199–220, September.

Jo, Eun Seo and Timnit Gebru. 2020. Lessons from archives: Strategies for collecting sociocultural data in machine learning. In *Proceedings of the 2020 conference on fairness, accountability, and transparency*, pages 306–316.

Kars, Marjoleine. 2020. *Blood on the River: A Chronicle of Mutiny and Freedom on the Wild Coast*. The New Press, New York City, New York, United Staes.

Kotek, Hadas, Rikker Dockum, and David Sun. 2023. Gender bias and stereotypes in large language models. In *Proceedings of The ACM Collective Intelligence Conference*, pages 12–24.

Luthra, Mrinalini, Konstantin Todorov, Charles Jeurgens, and Giovanni Colavizza. 2023. Unsilencing colonial archives via automated entity recognition. *Journal of Documentation*.

Meersbergen, Guido van. 2017. Writing east india company history after the cultural turn: Interdisciplinary perspectives on the seventeenth-century east india company and verenigde oostindische compagnie. *Journal for Early Modern Cultural Studies*, 17(3):10–36.

Naregal, Veena. 1999. Colonial bilingualism and hierarchies of language and power: Making of a vernacular sphere in western india. *Economic and Political Weekly*, pages 3446–3456.

Nath, Abhijnan, Sina Mahdipour Saravani, Ibrahim Khebour, Sheikh Mannan, Zihui Li, and Nikhil Krishnaswamy. 2022. A generalized method for automated multilingual loanword detection. In Calzolari, Nicoletta, Chu-Ren Huang, Hansaem Kim, James Pustejovsky, Leo Wanner, Key-Sun Choi, Pum-Mo Ryu, Hsin-Hsi Chen, Lucia Donatelli, Heng Ji, Sadao Kurohashi, Patrizia Paggio, Nianwen Xue, Seokhwan Kim, Younggyun Hahm, Zhong He, Tony Kyungil Lee, Enrico Santus, Francis Bond, and Seung-Hoon Na, editors, *Proceedings of the 29th International Conference on Computational Linguistics*, pages 4996–5013, Gyeongju, Republic of Korea, October. International Committee on Computational Linguistics.

Nationaal Archief. n.d. VOC: Opvarenden, 1699 - 1794.

Noble, Safiya Umoja. 2018. Algorithms of oppression: How search engines reinforce racism. In *Algorithms of oppression*. New York University Press.

Omiye, Jesutofunmi A., Jenna C. Lester, Simon Spichak, Veronica Rotemberg, and Roxana Daneshjou. 2023. Large language models propagate race-based medicine. *npj Digital Medicine*, 6(1):195, October.

Patterson, Orlando. 2018. *Slavery and social death: A comparative study, with a new preface*. Harvard University Press.

Peletz, Michael G. 2009. *Gender Pluralism: Southeast Asia Since Early Modern Times*. Routledge.

Pepping, K., H. Vellinga, M. Kuruppath, L. Van Wissen, and M. Van Rossum. 2023. GLOBALISE Thesaurus - Commodities.

Pepping, K. W. 2024. Reflections on language tagging: working with the multilingual dimension of the Dutch East India Company archives. *Journal of Open Humanities Data*, 10(29):1–10.

Petram, Lodewijk and Matthias van Rossum. 2022. Transforming historical research practices – a digital infrastructure for the voc archives (globalise). *International Journal of Maritime History*, 34(3):494–502.

Pinney, Christine, Amifa Raj, Alex Hanna, and Michael D. Ekstrand. 2023. Much ado about gender: Current practices and future recommendations for appropriate gender-aware information access. In *Proceedings of the 2023 Conference on Human Information Interaction and Retrieval*, CHIIR '23, page 269–279, New York, NY, USA. Association for Computing Machinery.

Prates, Marcelo O. R., Pedro H. Avelar, and Luís C. Lamb. 2020. Assessing gender bias in machine translation: a case study with google translate. *Neural Comput. Appl.*, 32(10):6363–6381, may.

Reddy, Gayatri. 2005. *With Respect to Sex: Negotiating Hijra Identity in South India*. University of Chicago Press, Chicago, IL, July.

Saunders, Danielle and Katrina Olsen. 2023. Gender, names and other mysteries: Towards the ambiguous for gender-inclusive translation. In Vanmassenhove, Eva, Beatrice Savoldi, Luisa Bentivogli, Joke Daems, and Janiça Hackenbuchner, editors, *Proceedings of the First Workshop on Gender-Inclusive Translation Technologies*, pages 85–93. European Association for Machine Translation.

Saunders, Danielle, Rosie Sallis, and Bill Byrne. 2020. Neural machine translation doesn't translate gender coreference right unless you make it. In Costa-jussà, Marta R., Christian Hardmeier, Will Radford, and Kellie Webster, editors, *Proceedings of the Second Workshop on Gender Bias in Natural Language Processing*, pages 35–43, Barcelona, Spain (Online), December. Association for Computational Linguistics.

Savoldi, Beatrice, Marco Gaido, Luisa Bentivogli, Matteo Negri, and Marco Turchi. 2021. Gender bias in machine translation. *Transactions of the Association for Computational Linguistics*, 9:845–874.

Scott, Joan W. 1986. Gender: A useful category of historical analysis. *The American Historical Review*, 91(5):1053–1075.

Scott, Joan Wallach. 2010. Gender: Still a useful category of analysis? *Diogenes*, 57(1):7–14.

Spivak, Gayatri Chakravorty. 1985. The rani of sirmur: An essay in reading the archives. *History and theory*, 24(3):247–272.

Stahlberg, Dagmar, Friederike Braun, Lisa Irmen, and Sabine Sczesny. 2007. Representation of the sexes. In Fiedler, Klaus, editor, *Social Communication*, pages 163–187. Psychology Press.

Stoler, Ann Laura. 2008. *Along the archival grain: Epistemic anxieties and colonial common sense*. Princeton University Press.

Stoler, Ann Laura. 2010. *Carnal Knowledge and Imperial Power: Race and the Intimate in Colonial Rule, With a New Preface*. University of California Press, Berkeley, Los Angeles, United States; London, United Kingdom.

Trouillot, Michel-Rolph. 2015. *Silencing the past: Power and the production of history*. Beacon Press.

Tudhope, Douglas and Marianne Lykke Nielsen. 2006. Introduction to knowledge organization systems and services. *New Review of Hypermedia and multimedia*, 12(1):3–9.

Vanmassenhove, Eva, Christian Hardmeier, and Andy Way. 2018. Getting gender right in neural machine translation. In Riloff, Ellen, David Chiang, Julia Hockenmaier, and Jun'ichi Tsujii, editors, *Proceedings of the 2018 Conference on Empirical Methods in Natural Language Processing*, pages 3003–3008, Brussels, Belgium, October-November. Association for Computational Linguistics.

Verkijk, Stella and Piek Vossen. 2023. Sunken ships shan't sail: Ontology design for reconstructing events in the dutch east india company archives. In *CEUR Workshop Proceedings*, pages 320–332. CEUR Workshop Proceedings.

Wamelen, Carla van. 2014. *Family life onder de VOC: Een handelscompagnie in huwelijks- en gezinszaken*. Uitgeverij Verloren.

Yusra, Kamaludin, Yuni Budi Lestari, and Jane Simpson. 2023. Borrowing of address forms for dimensions of social relation in a contact-induced multilingual community. *Journal of Politeness Research: Language, Behavior, Culture*, 19(1):217–248.

Zijlstra, Suzanne. 2021. *De voormoeders: een verborgen Nederlandse-Indische familiegeschiedenis*. Ambo Anthos, Amsterdam, The Netherlands.

# Pilot testing gender-inclusive translations and machine translations for German quadball referee certification test takers

**Joke Daems**
Ghent University
joke.daems@ugent.be
International Quadball Association
joke.daems@iqasport.org

## Abstract

Gender-inclusive translations are the default at the International Quadball Association, yet translators make different choices for the (timed) referee certification tests to improve readability. However, the actual impact of a strategy on readability and performance has not been tested. This pilot study explores the impact of translation strategy (masculine generic, gender-inclusive, and machine translation) on the speed, performance and perceptions of quadball referee test takers in German. It shows promise for inclusive over masculine strategies, and suggests limited usefulness of MT in this context.

## 1 Introduction

While the inherent importance of gender-inclusive language is clear (Sczesny et al., 2021), a commonly heard argument against the use of gender-inclusive language strategies is that they negatively impact readability and comprehensibility. With some notable exceptions (Friedrich et al., 2021), however, this impact has not been empirically tested.

At the International Quadball Association (IQA), gender-inclusive language is of critical importance, given the sports' commitment to gender inclusivity. While IQA translators aim to produce gender-inclusive translations, the desire for readability can outweigh the desire for inclusivity, particularly in the context of timed assessment for the referee certification tests (Daems, 2023)[1]. The German IQA translation team currently uses the colon as the non-binary marker in most translations, which also seems to be the strategy preferred by professional translators (Paolucci et al., 2023). This pilot study was conducted to answer the following research questions about referee certification test takers in German:

- Does inclusive language lead to slower answer times than generic masculine?
- Does inclusive language lead to lower test scores than generic masculine?
- Is machine translation (MT) a viable alternative when there are no translators available, considering answer time and test scores?
- What are test takers' perceptions about the understandability, readability, speed, and correctness of different conditions?

## 2 Methodology

A survey was created in Qualtrics (Qualtrics, Provo, UT) and distributed in April and May 2024. The main test block was randomised so as to evenly present the three conditions - gender-inclusive, generic masculine, and machine translation - to participants. It consisted of 14 multiple-choice questions taken from the official referee tests. Only questions with multiple references to people were selected to guarantee differences between the conditions. Questions were translated by IQA translators into the generic masculine and the gender-inclusive variant. For MT, each question and answer was translated using DeepL (translations generated in April 2024).



[1]Referees need to be certified to serve during official IQA games. Certification tests are created and hosted by the IQA and can be taken online at any time via https://hub.iqasport.org/



*Proceedings of the 2nd International Workshop on Gender-Inclusive Translation Technologies*, pages 56–57
June 27, 2024 ©2024 European Association for Machine Translation

At the end of the survey, participants were asked how strongly they agreed with the following statements: "I could understand the questions and answers", "I found it easy to read the questions and answers", "I answered the questions as fast as I would in a real referee test", and "I answered most questions correctly" (Likert scale of 1 = "Not at all" to 5 = "Completely").

Twenty-four valid survey responses were collected (eight for each condition). All participants were native German-speaking quadball players, and all but one were currently or soon to be certified referees. Statistical analyses were conducted using Microsoft Excel (ANOVA) and RStudio (linear mixed effects models), but no statistical differences were found between conditions so only descriptive numbers are presented here.

## 3 Results

**Speed**: Surprisingly, test takers were fastest in the inclusive condition, despite the text being 8% longer than the masculine condition (Table 1).

| condition | mean | median | stdev | min | max |
|---|---|---|---|---|---|
| **inclusive** | 378 | 396 | 110 | 182 | 551 |
| **masculine** | 465 | 453 | 144 | 216 | 780 |
| **MT** | 460 | 495 | 144 | 231 | 706 |

**Table 1:** Descriptive statistics for total time needed to answer all 14 questions (in seconds) per condition.

Reading speed is especially high for correctly answered questions in that condition (Figure 1).

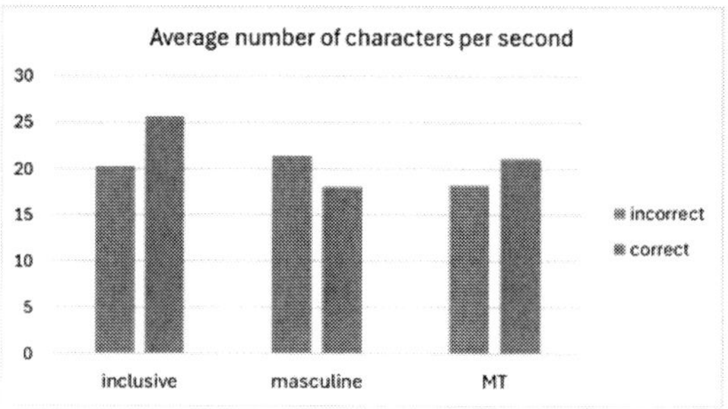


**Figure 1:** Average number of characters per second for the three conditions for questions answered incorrectly and correctly (excluding 'I don't know').

**Performance**: Participants in the inclusive condition scored highest on the test (Table 2), followed by those in the generic masculine condition.

**Perceptions**: MT scores worst overall (Figure 2). The inclusive condition scored highest on understandability and perceived correctness.

| condition | mean | median | stdev | min | max |
|---|---|---|---|---|---|
| **inclusive** | 10 | 10 | 2,1 | 6 | 13 |
| **masculine** | 9 | 8 | 3 | 5 | 13 |
| **MT** | 7,8 | 9 | 2,2 | 3 | 9 |

**Table 2:** Descriptive statistics for test scores per condition, max score = 14.

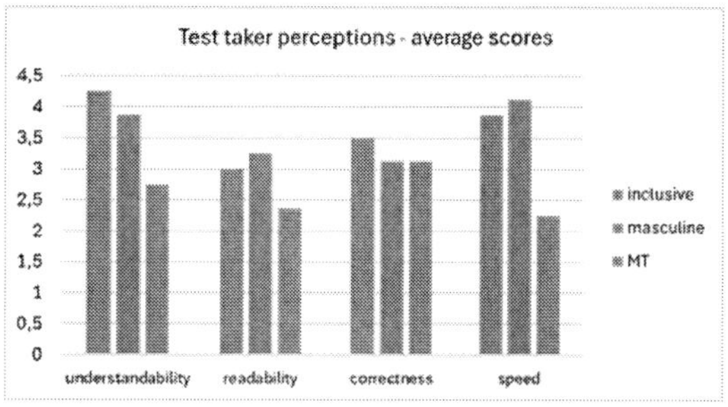


**Figure 2:** Average test taker perceptions per condition.

## 4 Conclusion & Future Work

Results suggest that (contrary to oft-heard criticism) speed and test scores are actually highest for the inclusive condition, showing its potential going forward. Based on the pilot study findings and participant feedback, MT is not currently seen as a viable strategy for referee test translation. Given the small sample size, statistically significant differences could not be identified, so for future work, we will expand this work by creating two variants (gender-inclusive and generic masculine) of the official IQA referee tests, in order to collect data from the entire population of referee test takers in a real-life setting.

## References

Daems, Joke. 2023. Gender-inclusive translation for a gender-inclusive sport: Strategies and translator perceptions at the in-ternational quadball association. In *Proceedings of the First Workshop on Gender-Inclusive Translation Technologies*, page 37–47.

Friedrich, Marcus C. G., Veronika Drößler, Nicole Oberlehberg, and Elke Heise. 2021. The influence of the gender asterisk ("genderstern-chen") on comprehensibility and interest. *Frontiers in Psychology*.

Paolucci, Angela Balducci, Manuel Lardelli, and Dagmar Gromann. 2023. Gender-fair language in translation: A case study. In *Proceedings of the First Workshop on Gender-Inclusive Translation Technologies*, page 13–23.

Sczesny, Sabine, Franziska Moser, and Wendy Wood. 2021. Beyond sexist beliefs: How do people decide to use gender-inclusive language? *Personality and Social Psychology Bulletin*, 41(7):943–954.

# Author Index

**Association for Computational Linguistics**
209 N. Eighth Street
Stroudsburg, Pennsylvania 18360

ISBN 979-8-3313-0479-9

9 798331 304799

CURRAN ASSOCIATES INC.
proceedings.com